北京高等教育精品教材

英语时文泛读（第2册）

Current News Articles for Extensive Reading

总主编　范守义
主　编　张　蕾　吴晓萍

北京大学出版社
PEKING UNIVERSITY PRESS

图书在版编目(CIP)数据

英语时文泛读(第2册)/范守义总主编.—北京:北京大学出版社,2009.4
(21世纪英语专业系列教材)
ISBN 978-7-301-14511-1

Ⅰ.英…　Ⅱ.范…　Ⅲ.英语－阅读教学－高等学校－教材　Ⅳ.H319.4

中国版本图书馆CIP数据核字(2009)第053939号

书　　　名：英语时文泛读(第2册)
著作责任者：范守义　总主编
组 稿 编 辑：张　冰
责 任 编 辑：刘　爽
标 准 书 号：ISBN 978-7-301-14511-1/H・2138
出 版 发 行：北京大学出版社
地　　　址：北京市海淀区成府路205号　100871
网　　　址：http://www.pup.cn　电子信箱:zpup@pup.pku.edu.cn
电　　　话：邮购部 62752015　发行部 62750672　编辑部 62754382　出版部 62754962
印　刷　者：北京虎彩文化传播有限公司
经　销　者：新华书店
　　　　　　787毫米×1092毫米　16开本　7.5印张　190千字
　　　　　　2009年4月第1版　2022年8月第9次印刷
定　　　价：36.00元

未经许可,不得以任何方式复制或抄袭本书之部分或全部内容。
版权所有,侵权必究
举报电话：(010)62752024　电子信箱:fd@pup.pku.edu.cn

本书荣获
"李嘉诚学术基金"资助

总　序

　　北京大学出版社自2005年以来已出版"语言与应用语言学知识系列读本"多种，为了配合第十一个五年计划，现又策划陆续出版《21世纪英语专业系列教材》。这个重大举措势必受到英语专业广大教师和学生的欢迎。

　　作为英语教师，最让人揪心的莫过于听人说英语不是一个专业，只是一个工具。说这些话的领导和教师的用心是好的，为英语专业的毕业生将来找工作着想，因此要为英语专业的学生多多开设诸如新闻、法律、国际商务、经济、旅游等其他专业的课程。但事与愿违，英语专业的教师们很快发现，学生投入英语学习的时间少了，掌握英语专业课程知识甚微，即使对四个技能的掌握也并不比大学英语学生高明多少，而那个所谓的第二专业在有关专家的眼中只是学到些皮毛而已。

　　英语专业的路在何方？有没有其他路可走？这是需要我们英语专业教师思索的问题。中央领导关于创新是一个民族的灵魂和要培养创新人才等的指示精神，让我们在层层迷雾中找到了航向。显然，培养学生具有自主学习能力和能进行创造性思维是我们更为重要的战略目标，使英语专业的人才更能适应21世纪的需要，迎接21世纪的挑战。

　　如今，北京大学出版社外语编辑室的领导和编辑同志们也从教材出版的视角探索英语专业的教材问题，从而为贯彻英语专业教学大纲做些有益的工作，为教师们开设大纲中所规定的必修、选修课程提供各种教材。"21世纪英语专业系列教材"是普通高等教育"十一五"国家级规划教材和国家"十一五"重点出版规划项目"面向新世纪的立体化网络化英语学科建设丛书"的重要组成部分。这套系列教材要体现新世纪英语教学的自主化、协作化、模块化和超文本化，结合外语教材的具体情况，既要解决教学内容、教学方法和教育技术的时代化，也要坚持弘扬以爱国主义为核心的民族精神。因此，今天北京大学出版社在大力提倡专业英语教学改革的基础上，编辑出版各种英语专业技能、英语专业知识和相关专业知识课程的教材，以培养具有创新性思维和具有实际工作能力的学生，充分体现了时代精神。

北京大学出版社的远见卓识，也反映了英语专业广大师生盼望已久的心愿。由北京大学等全国几十所院校具体组织力量，积极编写相关教材。这就是说，这套教材是由一些高等院校有水平有经验的第一线教师们制定编写大纲，反复讨论，特别是考虑到在不同层次、不同背景学校之间取得平衡，避免了先前的教材或偏难或偏易的弊病。与此同时，一批知名专家教授参与策划和教材审定工作，保证了教材质量。

当然，这套系列教材出版只是初步实现了出版社和编者们的预期目标。为了获得更大效果，希望使用本系列教材的教师和同学不吝指教，及时将意见反馈给我们，使教材更加完善。

航道已经开通，我们有决心乘风破浪，奋勇前进！

胡壮麟
北京大学蓝旗营

写给本书使用者的话

21世纪的中国是改革向广度和深度进军的世纪，21世纪的世界是全球化走向优化整合和更高水平的世纪。中国与世界各国交往向全方位推进和巩固是历史发展之必然。走在历史发展最前沿的是双语或多语工作者；而在当今的世界上，英语使用之广泛是举世公认的。中国的外语教育中英语是最为重要的外国语言。外交学院作为外语类院校在过去的半个多世纪中为中国外交外事和各个部门培养了大批外语人才，他们在各个领域发挥了巨大作用，做出了杰出的贡献。

外交学院是具有外交特色和外语优势的重点大学，外交学院的英语教学在复校后的30年中，积累了丰富的教学经验。"英语时文泛读"是外交学院英语本科教学的核心课程；该课程为学生提高英语阅读水平，增加词汇量和阅读技巧，丰富文化和国际知识提供了很好的学习平台。学习这门课程以及其他相关课程，可为学生走向职场奠定坚实的基础。外交学院培养出的学生具有国际视野和外交外事专业水准是十分恰当的评价。

2005年以来外交学院英语系将"英语泛读"作为精品项目立项，2007年夏被评为北京市精品课程；目前我们正在向国家级精品课程努力。该精品课程由两大板块组成，即课堂教学和课外阅读——课堂教学使用了精选的时文作为主要的教学内容；课外阅读使用了精选的英语简易读物、注释读物和英语原著作为主要内容，并为每一部书设计了100个问题，可以在计算机网络上进行在线测试，并立即得到结果，同时教师也能够立即看到全部参加测试者的成绩以及学生学期和学年的累计成绩。我们与北京外国语大学英语学院和首都师范大学外国语学院英语系合作，进行异地登录测试也取得了满意的结果。这种英语泛读课程创新的教学模式为迅速提高学生的英语水平和综合运用能力起到了很好的作用，深受教师和学生的欢迎。

这里我们主要谈一下课堂用书《英语时文泛读》的编辑情况。

我们的编写设计思路如下：

1. 所选文本要语言地道，内容新颖（除个别为略早的文章，其余课文全部为2005年以后英美主要报刊杂志上发表的文章），题材广泛多样（涉及政治、经济、文化、教育、科技、环保、法律、社会等诸方面内容），贴近时代与生活，易激发学生兴趣。

2. 该教材就不同主题设不同单元，知识内容较成体系，既有助于学生系统学习、积累和运用所学知识，又有助于学生分类学习记忆相关词汇。

3. 练习设计合理、实用，既有很强的针对性（针对每个单元具体的阅读技巧及目标），又能考察学生的综合能力，形式比较灵活，易于操作。

4. 为使所选用的文本难度符合学生的英语程度，既不要过易，也不要过难，我们根据美国著名教育家鲁道夫·弗莱什(Rudolf Flesch)博士的研究理论，即"英语文章难易度与单位长度的音节数和词数密切相关"，将其数学模型化，并在其基础上编写的程序，进行《英语时文泛读》文本的选材，剔除了过难和过易的文本。

5. 编写旨在为使用《英语时文泛读》的教师准备的《教师参考书》，提供必要而丰富的备课参考资料和练习答案。

6. 制作课堂使用的PPT文档，供授课使用，教师亦可增添或删节内容，以适应具体需要。

7. 编辑快速阅读文本，以及相关的英国英语和美国英语的知识等内容，供教学参考使用。

8. 使用者可以根据本教学单位学生的英语水平，使用合适的单元和文本长度进行课堂阅读活动。

9. 为了锻炼学生自己查字典和确定词义的能力，在文本A和文本B的词汇表中，只给出没有在练习中出现的词；为照顾部分学生学习的需要，各单元的生词按英语字母表列在全书之后，学生可以查阅、记忆，然后再去做练习。

为保证教材编写的专业水准，我们组成了以范守义教授为负责人的《英语时文泛读》教程编写委员会，人员如下：

范守义：总主编，负责策划统筹、审阅和编辑等工作。

石毅、于倩：共同主编，负责《英语时文泛读》第一册的编写工作；

张蕾、吴晓萍：共同主编，负责《英语时文泛读》第二册的编写工作；

武波、王振玲：共同主编，负责《英语时文泛读》第三册的编写工作；

徐英、魏腊梅：共同主编，负责《英语时文泛读》第四册的编写工作。

我们期待《英语时文泛读》的出版能够为我国大学本科和程度相当的英语学习者提供一套新的泛读教程，以满足与时俱进的教学要求；为此我们期待广大教师和学生提出宝贵意见和要求，以改进我们的编写工作。我们也期待以《英语时文泛读》为主和能进行在线测试的课外阅读为辅的创新英语泛读教学模式为推动和提升全国泛读教学做出贡献。

《英语时文泛读》教程编写委员会

2008年9月26日

目 录
CONTENTS

UNIT ONE   **THE IMPACT OF GLOBALIZATION**   *1*

     Text A   A Year Without "Made in China" / 1

     Text B   Stay Globally Competitive: Be Like Google / 7

     Text C   A Race We Can All Win / 11

UNIT TWO   **CONTROVERSIES IN 21ST-CENTURY AMERICA**   *14*

     Text A   Why Not Teach Alternatives to Evolution? / 14

     Text B   Don't Believe the Hype. We're Still No.1. / 20

     Text C   Supreme Court Rejects School Racial Diversity Plans / 24

UNIT THREE   **COLLEGE AND RESPONSIBILITY**   *29*

     Text A   What Exactly Does GW's President Do? / 29

     Text B   Campuses Slow to Deal with Growth in Gambling / 34

     Text C   Gates Urges Graduates to Tackle Global Inequity / 39

UNIT FOUR   **"NEW" GENERATIONS**   *43*

     Text A   What Gen Y Really Wants / 43

     Text B   What Will You Call Me When I'm 64? / 48

     Text C   Why We Must Listen to Our Angry Teenagers / 52

| **UNIT FIVE** | **PARADOXES IN REALITY** | **56** |

Text A The Cleanest Place on Earth—and the Dirtiest / 56

Text B Somewhere Deep Down, We Still Care. Don't We? / 61

Text C Could Friendships Be Ruining Your Life? / 66

| **UNIT SIX** | **PEOPLE'S PLACE IN SOCIETY** | **71** |

Text A Setting Happiness as a National Goal / 71

Text B When Armed Citizens Patrol the Streets / 75

Text C Designing Cities for People, Rather than Cars... / 80

| **UNIT SEVEN** | **HUMAN IMPACT ON NATURE** | **84** |

Text A After We Are Gone / 84

Text B A New Step Toward Synthetic Life / 90

Text C Can We Save the World by 2015? / 95

GLOSSARY / 99

UNIT ONE

THE IMPACT OF GLOBALIZATION

Target of the Unit

☞ To get a glimpse of the impact of globalization on business, nations and ordinary people's lives
☞ To practice reading skills
☞ To enlarge your vocabulary

1) LEAD IN

Directions: In this unit, you will read 3 passages about the advantages and disadvantages brought about by globalization. Read them critically and see whether you agree with the ideas expressed in them.

2) DISCUSSION

What is globalization? What advantages and disadvantages has it brought to our lives?

Text A

A Year Without "Made in China"

By Sara Bongiorni

Warming-up Exercises

☞ How do you feel about the fact that China has virtually become the factory of the world?
☞ What is your overall impression of products made in China?

• First reading •

Directions: Now please read the following passage as fast as you can and summarize the main idea.

1　　BATON ROUGE, LA. — Last year, two days after Christmas, we kicked China out of the house. Not the country obviously, but bits of plastic, metal, and wood stamped with the words "Made in China." We kept what we already had, but stopped bringing any more in.

2　　The banishment was no fault of China's. It had coated our lives with a cheerful **veneer** of toys, gadgets, and $10 children's shoes. Sometimes I worried about jobs sent overseas, but price trumped virtue at our house. We couldn't resist what China was selling.

3　　But on that dark Monday last year, a creeping unease washed over me as I sat on the sofa and surveyed the gloomy **wreckage** of the holiday. It wasn't until then that I noticed an irrefutable fact: China was taking over the place.

4　　It stared back at me from the empty screen of the television. I spied it in the pile of tennis shoes by the door. It glowed in the lights on the Christmas tree and watched me in the eyes of a doll **splayed** on the floor. I slipped off the couch and did a quick **inventory**, sorting gifts into two stacks: China and non-China. The count came to China, 25, the world, 14. Christmas, I realized, had become a holiday made by the Chinese. Suddenly I'd had enough. I wanted China out.

5　　Through tricks and persuasion I got my husband on board, and on Jan. 1 we launched a yearlong household **embargo** on Chinese imports. The idea wasn't to punish China, which would never feel the **pinprick** of our protest. And we didn't fool ourselves into thinking we'd bring back a single job to **unplugged** company towns in Ohio and Georgia. We pushed China out of our lives because we wanted to measure how far

veneer *n.* superficial appearance covering/disguising the true nature of sb/sth 虚假的表象
wreckage *n.* remains of sth that has been wrecked or ruined（被毁坏之物）残骸
splay *v.* to spread apart widely, or to make things, esp parts of the body, do this（尤指四肢）伸展开
inventory *n.* detailed list, eg of goods, furniture, jobs to be done 清单
embargo *n.* official order that forbids sth, esp trade, the movement of ships, etc 禁运
pinprick *n.* sth that slightly annoys sb 小烦恼
unplugged (company town) *adj.* A lot of small towns, especially in the more rural parts of the country, have only one major factory/company located nearby. These towns become very dependent on said companies, and when they move out overseas, it can be devastating for the town and surrounding areas. So, it just basically means a town that had "the" factory ripped/jerked/unplugged from the community, and has suffered a great deal.（支柱企业）彻底搬迁走的（城镇）

it had pushed in. We wanted to know what it would take in time, money, and **aggravation** to kick our China habit.

6 We hit the first **rut** in the road when I discovered our son's toes pressing against the ends of his tennis shoes. I wore myself out hunting for new ones. After two weeks I broke down and spent $60 on sneakers from Italy. I felt sick over the money; it seemed decadent for a pair of children's shoes. I got used to the feeling. Weeks later I shelled out $60 for Texas-made shoes for our toddler daughter.

7 We got hung up on lots of little things. I drove to half a dozen grocery stores in search of candles for my husband's birthday cake, eventually settling on a box of dusty leftovers I found in the kitchen. The junk drawer has been stuck shut since January. My husband found the part to fix it at Home Depot but left it on the shelf when he spotted the telltale "Made in China."

8 Mini crises erupted when our **blender** and television broke down. The television **sputtered** back to life without intervention, but it was a long, hot summer without **smoothies**. We killed four mice with old-fashioned snapping traps because the catch-and-release ones we prefer are made in China. Last summer at the beach my husband wore a pair of mismatched **flip-flops** my mother found in her garage. He'd run out of options at the drug store.

9 Navigating the toy aisle has been a **wilting** affair. In the spring, our 4-year-old son launched a countercampaign in support of "China things." He's been a good sport, but he's weary of Danish-made Legos, the only sure bet for birthday gifts for his friends. One morning in October he fell apart during a trip to Target when he developed a sudden lust for an electric purple pumpkin. "It's too long without China," he wailed. He kept at me all day.

10 The next morning I drove him back so he could use his birthday money to buy the pumpkin for himself. I kept my fingers off the bills as he passed them to the checker.

11 My husband bemoans the Christmas gifts he can't buy because they were made in China. He plans to sew sleeping bags for the children himself. He can build wooden boats and guitars, but I fear he will meet his match with thread and needle. "How hard can it

---

aggravation n. annoyance; irritation 激怒，惹恼
rut n. deep track made by a wheel or wheels in soft ground; furrow 车辙
blender n. liquidizer 榨汁机
sputter v. to make short soft uneven noises like very small explosions 发出噼噼啪啪声
smoothie n. a thick drink made of fruit and fruit juices mixed together, sometimes with ice, milk and yoghurt 以水果、果汁及牛奶或酸奶混合而成的浓稠饮品
flip-flops n. In footwear and fashion, flip-flops (also known as thongs, jandals, slippers, or pluggers) are a flat, backless, usually rubber sandal consisting of a flat sole held loosely on the foot by a Y-shaped strap, like a thin thong, that passes between the first (big) and second toes and around either side of the foot. They appear to have been developed based on traditional Japanese woven or wooden soled sandals. 夹趾拖鞋
wilt v. (infml) to feel weak or tired, esp because one is too hot (因天热而)发蔫，感觉疲惫

be?" he scoffed.

12   The funny thing about China's ascent is that we, as a nation, could shut the whole thing down in a week. Jump-start a "Just Say No to Chinese Products Week," and the

> **scoff** v. to speak contemptuously (about or to sb/sth); jeer or mock 嘲弄，嘲笑
> **jump-start** v. to help a process or activity to start or become more successful 助推，发起
> **cargo** n. (load of) goods carried in a ship or aircraft (船/飞机运载的)货物(量)

empire will collapse amid the chaos of overloaded cargo ships in Long Beach harbor. I doubt we could pull it off. Americans may be famously patriotic, but look closely, and you'll see who makes the flag magnets on their car bumpers. These days China delivers every major holiday, Fourth of July included.

13   I don't know what we will do after Dec. 31 when our family's embargo comes to its official end. China-free living has been a hassle. I have discovered for myself that China doesn't control every aspect of our daily lives, but if you take a close look at the underside of boxes in the toy department, I promise it will give you pause.

14   Our son knows where he stands on the matter. In the bathtub one evening he told me how happy he was that "the China season" was coming soon. "When we can buy China things again, let's never stop," he said.

15   After a year without China I can tell you this: You can still live without it, but it's getting trickier and costlier by the day. And a decade from now I may not be brave enough to try it again.

(Words: 957)

• Second Reading •

Directions: Read the text again more carefully to find enough information for Exercises I, II & III.

Exercise I True or False

Directions: Please state whether the following statements are true or not (T/F) according to the text.

1. The author's family had bought a lot of products made in China because of their competitive prices.

2. The author realized one day that Chinese goods had gained control of her house.
3. Then she decided to refuse to buy goods imported from China for ever.
4. Their household embargo on Chinese imports was aimed to punish China.
5. Children's shoes made elsewhere are usually much more expensive than those made in China.
6. All candles for birthday cakes available at the grocery stores seemed to be made in China.
7. Her husband had to wear a pair of mismatched old flip-flops because there were no shoes of his size available at the store.
8. She bought her son an electric pumpkin which was not made in China.
9. Now Chinese products have become indispensable to all major American holidays including the Independence Day.
10. This yearlong experiment proved that life could get harder without stuff made in China.

Exercise II Word Inference

Directions: Often you can guess the meaning of a word/expression by reading the words around it. Please read the given sentence to see how each word/expression in bold type is used in the text. Then choose the answer that is closest in meaning to the bold-faced word/expression.

1. The **banishment** was no fault of China's.
   A. exile   B. removal   C. exclusion   D. punishment
2. It wasn't until then that I noticed an **irrefutable** fact: China was taking over the place.
   A. unlikely   B. obvious   C. hidden   D. indisputable
3. I **spied** it in the pile of tennis shoes by the door.
   A. noticed   B. kept watching secretly
   C. watched closely   D. guarded against
4. I felt sick over the money; it seemed **decadent** for a pair of children's shoes.
   A. meaningless
   B. having low moral standards
   C. reasonable
   D. having high moral standards

5. Weeks later I **shelled out** $60 for Texas-made shoes for our toddler daughter.

   A. paid out reluctantly

   B. spent generously

   C. used up

   D. saved

6. My husband found the part to fix it at Home Depot but left it on the shelf when he spotted the **telltale** "Made in China."

   A. storytelling   B. interesting   C. telling   D. lying

7. He's been **a good sport**, but he's weary of Danish-made Legos, the only sure bet for birthday gifts for his friends.

   A. a pleasant, cheerful and helpful person

   B. a good sportsman

   C. a sports fan

   D. a good friend

8. My husband **bemoans** the Christmas gifts he can't buy because they were made in China.

   A. shows sorrow for   B. complains about

   C. criticizes   D. desires

9. The funny thing about China's **ascent** is that we, as a nation, could shut the whole thing down in a week.

   A. development   B. upward path

   C. climbing up   D. rise

10. China-free living has been a **hassle**.

    A. argument   B. goal

    C. difficulty   D. great joy

Exercise III   Discussion

Directions: Please discuss the following questions in pairs or groups.

1. What might be the reasons that made products made in China so ubiquitous even in the USA?

2. Do you think the author's worries about China's growing economic influence are justifiable? Why/why not?

Text B

Stay Globally Competitive: Be Like Google

By Peter Georgescu

Warming-up Exercises

☞ What do you know about Google?
☞ What features or advantages does it require to remain globally competitive in the 21st century?

• First reading •

Directions: Now please read the following passage as fast as you can and summarize the main idea.

1   The war between consumers and producers is over. Consumers won. For decades the economic world order was dominated by excess demand. Scarce resources, including capital, were the **differentiators** between winners and losers.

2   But by the beginning of this decade consumers began to see, in almost every category, a **plethora** of products and services that looked, felt, and performed alike. Goods that were once hard to get became readily available and affordable, putting the decision-making power firmly in the hands of the consumer.

3   ___A___. Commoditization—what I see as the cancer of 21st-century commerce—has fueled **ferocious** price competition, leading to lower prices, **margins**, and profits for businesses. With

> **differentiator** *n.* sth that distinguishes one thing/person from the other 区分者，差别指数
> **plethora** *n.* quantity greater than what is needed; over-abundance 过量，过剩
> **ferocious** *adj.* fierce, violent or savage 残忍的，凶猛的，野蛮的
> **margin** *n.* difference between cost price and selling price 差价，利润
> **reinvigorate** *v.* to give a boost, revive 振兴，使重新获得活力

price as the only real differentiator, producers are left with a challenge: They must find a way to stand out in the crowd.

4   Unless you offer consumers something unique, the low-cost producers will win the battle every time. ___B___. As we look at the rise of India and China, or even a **reinvigorated** Europe, we must ask ourselves how America will compete in coming decades against powerful new

forces, probably bigger than us and capable of producing goods and services at significantly lower prices.

5   There's only one way to avoid the commodity quagmire, and it's not easy: It's through creativity.

widget *n.* an imaginary product that a company might produce 设想中的新装置/产品
adman *n.* （infml）a person who produces commercial advertisements 广告人
rung *n.* cross-piece forming a step in a ladder; level or rank in society, one's career, an organization, etc 梯级, 等级

6   The good news is that at their best, American business minds excel at putting creativity to work. In the past half-century, Americans created everything from the Post-it note to the artificial heart to the Internet. Today Steve Jobs and nearly everyone employed at Google let their imaginations loose as a matter of course.

7   Something new, it seems, is born at Google (Charts, Fortune 500) every week, making it the creative factory of this century and a model other companies should study carefully. It is a culture where innovation is not only nurtured but also expected and rewarded. (You probably haven't even heard of Google's Gadget Ads, a new option that allows advertisers to create interactive ads within **widgets**, or Google Shared Stuff, a feature that lets you share your favorite bookmarks with others. Both functions were added in recent weeks.)

8   ___C___. Absolutely. Google need not be the exception; it should become the norm. In my 30-plus years in the advertising business, I witnessed good writers become great, art directors turn into geniuses. I've seen midsized consulting companies teach top CEOs breakthrough management techniques that are in reality courses in creativity.

9   When I was working as an account manager on the United Negro College Fund campaign during the 1970s, I witnessed a young copy supervisor's transition from a decent writer to a brilliant **adman**. After digesting the research material and developing a strong understanding of the market he was trying to reach, he came up with a slogan that continues to resonate today: "A mind is a terrible thing to waste."___D___.

10   All these examples show that creativity can be taught or developed in the right environment.___E___. Creativity is almost never a logical process. Great ideas come from everywhere—from the lowest **rungs** on the corporate ladder to the chairman of the board. But a company needs to be organized in a manner whereby it can hear, capture, and develop fresh ideas when they are hatched.

11   It's not easy becoming the next Google—or GE, or 3M, or name your favorite powerhouse of imagination. But for anyone trying to compete in the coming decades, creativity is one process that can't be left for later.

(Words: 629)

Second Reading

Directions: Read the text again more carefully to find enough information for Exercises I, II, III, IV & V.

Exercise I Understanding Text Organization

Directions: You may find there are a few sentences (segments) missing from the passage. Read the article through and decide where the following sentences should go.

1. But if creativity is to be the differentiator of the decade, the larger question is, can creativity be learned?
2. Over three decades later, it's still used by the organization.
3. While this shift is good for consumers, it is leaving producers scrambling.
4. The hard part, of course, is actually teaching it.
5. Brand America is no exception.

Exercise II Multiple-Choice Questions

Directions: Please choose the best answer from the four choices given.

1. For decades in the past century, what really differentiated winners and losers in business seemed to be _____.
   A. price   B. scarce resources
   C. technology   D. information
2. The author sees _____ as the cancer of 21st-century commerce.
   A. price competition   B. lower prices
   C. excess demand   D. commoditization

3. _____ makes Google the creative factory of this century and a model of other companies.

   A. Steve Jobs
   B. Its innovation-oriented culture
   C. Google's Gadget Ads
   D. Google Shared Stuff

4. What is NOT true about creativity?

   A. It can be planned.
   B. It can be taught.
   C. It can be learned.
   D. It can be developed.

5. Which company is not mentioned as a model of creative companies?

   A. Google.   B. GE.   C. GM.   D. 3M.

Exercise III   Word Matching

Directions: Please choose the supplied words to explain the original forms of the boldfaced words in the following sentences.

A. a standard   B. echo   C. a difficult situation   D. compete   E. develop

1. While this shift is good for consumers, it is leaving producers **scrambling**.
2. There's only one way to avoid the commodity **quagmire**…
3. It is a culture where innovation is not only **nurtured** but also expected and rewarded.
4. Google need not be the exception; it should become the **norm**.
5. … he came up with a slogan that continues to **resonate** today…

Exercise IV   Short-Answer Questions

Directions: Please answer the following questions briefly in your own words.

1. In what way did consumers win the war?
2. How can a company beat its low-cost competitors?
3. What does the expression "let their imaginations loose" mean?

Exercise V   Discussion

Directions: Please discuss the following questions in pairs or groups.

1. What other examples can you cite to show that American business minds excel at putting creativity to work?
2. How can creativity and innovation be nurtured in a company and in a society?

Text C

A Race We Can All Win

By Michael Bloomberg

1   China's economic transformation over the past two decades is a fascinating, but still poorly understood, story. Many American politicians have played to voters' economic insecurities by scapegoating China, suggesting that the Chinese are the source of our problems and a threat to our prosperity. But based on my 35 years of experience in the private sector, and six years running the nation's largest city, I believe that China is not a threat to America, but an opportunity. An *incredible* opportunity.

2   While we should recognize that China and the United States are competitors, we should also understand that geopolitics and global economics are not zero-sum games. Just as a growing American economy is good for China, a growing Chinese economy is good for America. That means we have a stake in working together to solve common problems, rather than trying to browbeat or intimidate the other into action. And it means we should seize on opportunities to learn from one another.

3   In early December I met with business and government leaders in Beijing and Shanghai. It was not my first trip to those cities: the company I founded 25 years ago has built offices in 130 cities, including Beijing, Shanghai and Hong Kong. Over the years I've watched China emerge as an economic dynamo, but I've also seen the frailties underpinning its system. From a distance of 7,000 miles, it's easy to think that China is overflowing with success. But the picture on the ground is far more complicated.

4   When I landed at the Pudong airport near Shanghai on my recent visit, I rode the high-speed magnetic-levitation train that runs between the airport and the city: with a top speed of 268 miles per hour, it's far faster than any train in the United States. This high-tech train of the future symbolizes how Shanghai, with its rising skyscrapers and booming financial markets, is

working to rival New York as the city of the future.

5   But one of the chief reasons China built the maglev train—and why other countries like Japan are also developing maglev networks—was to help relieve their increasingly congested roads and increasingly polluted air. When you are in Shanghai or Beijing, it is impossible to escape either, and together, they threaten to choke the Chinese economy and its people. The growth of Chinese cities is also exposing other fundamental long-term economic challenges for China. For instance, China's education system is simply not producing enough skilled workers—engineers, doctors, scientists and managers—to meet the demands of its economy. At the same time, health-care costs are skyrocketing, which is causing rising financial anxiety among Chinese families.

6   Congestion. Pollution. Education concerns. Rising health-care costs. If this all sounds familiar, it should. In New York and across America, we face similar problems in all of these areas, but with all the hyperbole about China, it's easy to forget that we remain substantially ahead.

7   The challenge that we face is not preventing China from catching up with where we are today, but preventing ourselves from slowing down. That means overcoming the political inertia that has stopped us from investing in the 21st-century infrastructure that we need—not just high-speed rail lines but bigger ports, more mass-transit systems, more clean-energy capacity and more extensive broadband systems.

8   It also means overcoming widespread inertia in our efforts to improve the affordability of health care and the quality of education. In New York, we're proving that raising standards and holding schools and students accountable for results can lead to dramatic improvements in student achievement. America has the most advanced, cutting-edge universities in the world, driving innovation in every field. But to maintain that edge, we need a public-school system that is just as good, and that prepares our students to succeed in the new economy.

9   This summer's Olympic Games will give China a chance to showcase its impressive economic progress. But it will also remind the world that much work remains to be done in building a healthy society where differences of opinion—on politics, philosophy and faith—are respected as fundamental human rights. We live that lesson every day in New York, and as China may yet come to see, it is our greatest competitive advantage in the global economy.

(Words: 734)

Exercise I Discussion

Directions: Please discuss the following questions in pairs or groups.

1. Why is China being scapegoated frequently? For what problems of theirs are some westerners blaming China often?
2. According to Bloomberg, what strengths and weaknesses do China and the US have respectively?
3. What is the hidden message the author tries to convey? Do you agree with him?

Exercise II Writing

Directions: Write a letter of about 150 words to those worrying American consumers like Sara Bongiorni who might have a fear of the so-called "China threat," to assure them that China's growing economy is to bring about a win-win situation instead of a zero-sum game.

UNIT TWO

CONTROVERSIES IN 21ST-CENTURY AMERICA

Target of the Unit

☞ To learn about the conflicts between some old ideas and new ones in contemporary American life
☞ To practice reading skills
☞ To enlarge your vocabulary

1) LEAD IN

Directions: In this unit, you will read 3 passages about some controversial ideas and practices in contemporary American life, which are in fact the reflections of permanent conflicts between the old and the new in this society. Read critically and judge how they may impact the future of America.

2) DISCUSSION

Do you know any controversies in the contemporary American society? What's your opinion of such issues?

Text A

Why Not Teach Alternatives to Evolution?

By Gary Thompson et al

Warming-up Exercises

☞ Have you ever heard of Charles Darwin? What do you know about the theory of evolution?

• First reading •

Directions: Now please read the following passage as fast as you can and then get the exercises done as required.

1   USA TODAY's editorial calls "intelligent design" "**creationism** with clever new packaging." It would be an understatement to say this view is close-minded and ignorant. Creationism and intelligent design are not the same; their arguments do differ. ("Smart move in Dover," last Friday).

2   Why does USA TODAY think Dover's citizens, who voted out eight of nine school board members who had backed a statement regarding intelligent design, are wiser than Kansas school board members? The

> **creationism** *n.* the position that the account of the creation of the universe given at the beginning of the Bible is literally true 特创论：认为《圣经》篇首给出的创造宇宙的叙述是真实无误的学说
> **oxymoronic** *adj.* contradictory 自相矛盾的
> **dumb down** *v.phr.* (used to show disapproval) to present news or information in a simple and attractive way without many details so that everyone can understand it 为求通俗易懂而将内容简单化（用于表示不赞同）

Kansas school board voted to give kids an option to study the different views of how our universe was created or evolved. I'd argue that this will make Kansas students better thinkers and allow them to make decisions on their own. USA TODAY says evolution is the foundation for biology. But a theory is only speculation. Therefore, to say a theory is foundational seems a little **oxymoronic**, and not a very sturdy foundation. I am sure this debate will go on, but it's important to me that we be more open-minded about our existence and our beginnings. We owe it to our kids to give them every possible option to think on such matters. There is nothing intelligent about **dumbing down** our children's education.

—Gary Thompson, Mansfield, Ohio

Monopoly on what's godly?

3   After reading the Rev. Pat Robertson's comments regarding the school board election in Dover, Pa., I'd just like to say: This is one more reason why I am sick and tired of the religious right. Every single time one of their issues comes up—be it abortion or intelligent design or whatever—members of the religious right say their opponents

are against God. Where do Robertson and his friends get the gall to assert that they have the monopoly on what God does or does not stand for?

—*Jason Malin, Denver*

Maintain science's strengths

4 Kansas' board of education has approved a measure to challenge Charles Darwin and "change the state's definition of 'science,' no longer limiting it to a search for natural explanations of phenomena" ("Kansas schools can teach 'intelligent design,'" *Life*, Nov. 9). As a scientist, I feel the following points are critical:

5 First, science, as a discipline, welcomes challenges. This is how science evolves and seeks truth. It is the strength, not the weakness, of the scientific method that innumerable examples of "dogma" scientists believed to be true in the past have later been shown to be false.

6 Second, the **bar** must be raised for a new scientific explanation of a phenomenon to replace a prior one. It must be better at explaining and predicting natural events, and be verified through testing. Thus, the argument that the world is so complex that evolution can't explain it does nothing to replace an existing theory with an improved, testable explanation. As such, intelligent design will have no long-term sustainability as an alternative to evolution in the science classroom.

> **bar** *n.* a standard, expectation, or degree of requirement 标准
> **chalk sth up** *v.phr.* to record what one has done; to write sth down（usu with chalk）记录下来，记上一笔
> **perpetuate** *v.* to cause sth to continue 使(某事物)永久、永存或持续

7 Third, redefining science is a tremendous step backward in our technological society. If we, as a society, value eradication of disease and famine, the predicting of natural disasters, increasing public safety and ensuring a safe environment, then the objective, scientific method based on observation and testing must continue to be taught—undiluted. Should we learn nothing from Hurricane Katrina, and simply **chalk it up** as an "act of God"?

—*William S. Pietrzak, Ph.D., Warsaw, Ind.*

Evolution is "intelligent"

8 Why are evolution and intelligent design discussed as though they are mutually exclusive? To me, it seems obvious that evolution is "intelligent design." What could be more intelligent than designing a world that is self-sustaining, self-**perpetuating** and self-adjusting?

—*Robin Lara, Sierra Vista, Ariz.*

Kansas made "laughingstock"

9 As a former resident of Kansas, I am shocked and appalled that the Kansas board of education is again determined to make the Sunflower State the laughingstock of the world. This may be expected in the South, but Midwestern states are generally known for level-headedness. It's as though the school board has handed the world a big hammer and said, "Hit us in the head again, but hit us harder this time." There is nothing intelligent about intelligent design. This is a blatant attempt to replace science with religious dogma, and thinking with blind faith. The battle between scientific discovery and religious dogma is nothing new. When Galileo argued that the Earth was not the center of the universe, the church wanted him punished, and he spent the rest of his life under house arrest. When Charles Darwin made his great contribution to science, there were some religious fanatics who wanted him executed. To not believe in evolution is to believe that all life forms remain static.

—Russ Broadway, Sacramento

Kansas shows courage

10 No, Kansas, you are not a laughingstock. If they really seek to determine the truth, scientists are not afraid to follow where the evidential trail leads. Dismissing a "designer" because the concept is not a natural process assumes that the natural world is all there is. Hypothetically, if the supernatural does exist, the naturalist can never know the truth. But if the scientist begins with the possibility of the natural or supernatural and rigorously follows where the evidence leads, then he can have confidence that he has not omitted truth before he has even pulled out of his driveway. More and more, Darwinian evolution's trail has proved a weed-choked dead end. Kansas' school board has heard evidence from scientists—yes, real ones, Dorothy—that many folks refuse to hear or acknowledge. The board decided not that evolution be banned and intelligent design implemented, as the frothing news media love to portray, but that valid scientific theories, warts and all, ought to be assessed by its students. Kansas, you have shown great courage, willing to stand for truth despite the harangues of evolutionists and newspapers. Well done.

—Keith R. Pond, Wichita Falls, Texas

(Words: 972)

> **laughingstock** *n.* an object of jokes or ridicule; a butt 玩笑或嘲弄的对象，抨击的对象，笑柄
> **blatant** *adj.* very obvious; unashamed 明目张胆的
> **frothing** *adj.* producing froth; (infml) extremely angry 口吐白沫的，极其愤怒的
> **warts and all** *n.phr.* all defects and imperfections notwithstanding 尽管有各种缺点与瑕疵

Second Reading

Directions: Read the text again more carefully to find enough information for Exercises I, II & III.

Exercise I True or False

Directions: Please state whether the following statements are true or not (T/F) according to the text.

1. The article seems to maintain a neutral stand in the debate between "intelligent design" and evolution.
2. *USA TODAY* thinks Dover's citizens are wiser than Kansas school board members.
3. The Kansas school board vetoed the draft to give kids an option to study the different views of how the universe was created or evolved.
4. Gary Thompson believes kids should have their own options to think on such matters.
5. Jason Malin agrees with the ideas of the Rev. Pat Robertson.
6. It is the strength of science to welcome challenges.
7. As a scientist, William S. Pietrzak believes that teaching intelligent design as an alternative to evolution in the science classroom will not be sustainable.
8. Robin Lara argues that "intelligent design" and evolution are just the same.
9. Russ Broadway is a firm advocate for evolution.
10. Keith R. Pond supported the ban on teaching evolution in Kansas.

Exercise II Word Inference

Directions: Often you can guess the meaning of a word/expression by reading the words around it. Please read the given sentence to see how each word/expression in bold type is used in the text. Then choose the answer that is closest in meaning to the bold-faced word/expression.

1. It would be an **understatement** to say this view is close-minded and ignorant.
   A. underway   B. exaggeration   C. understating   D. overstatement
2. Where do Robertson and his friends get the **gall** to assert that they have the monopoly on what God does or does not stand for?
   A. idea   B. impudence   C. courage   D. resentment

3. It is the strength, not the weakness, of the scientific method that innumerable examples of "**dogma**" scientists believed to be true in the past have later been shown to be false.
   A. authoritative   B. principled   C. dictatorial   D. dogmatic
4. It must be better at explaining and predicting natural events, and be **verified** through testing.
   A. proved   B. certified   C. varied   D. examined
5. … then the objective, scientific method based on observation and testing must continue to be taught—**undiluted**.
   A. undoubted   B. mixed   C. pure   D. undisturbed
6. As a former resident of Kansas, I am shocked and **appalled** that the Kansas board of education is again determined to make the Sunflower State the laughingstock of the world.
   A. terrified   B. afraid   C. alerted   D. appealed
7. This may be expected in the South, but Midwestern states are generally known for **level-headedness**.
   A. having flat heads   B. having levelers
   C. sober-mindedness   D. ignorance
8. To not believe in evolution is to believe that all life forms remain **static**.
   A. motionless   B. permanent
   C. stable   D. unchanging
9. **Hypothetically**, if the supernatural does exist, the naturalist can never know the truth.
   A. Imaginarily   B. Supposedly
   C. Fictionally   D. In fact
10. Kansas, you have shown great courage, willing to stand for truth despite the **harangues** of evolutionists and newspapers.
    A. long angry speeches of criticism.   B. harassment
    C. threats   D. arguments

Exercise III Discussion

Directions: Please discuss the following questions in pairs or groups.

1. Do you believe in the theory of evolution? Why/why not?
2. The U.S. is known as the most advanced country worldwide, yet some of its public schools still teach "intelligent design." How do you think about such a paradoxical phenomenon?

Text B

Don't Believe the Hype. We're Still No. 1.

By Charles Krauthammer

Warming-up Exercises

☞ In what aspects does the U.S. lead the world?
☞ What do you think might make the Americans feel not so confident from time to time?

• First reading •

Directions: Now please read the following passage as fast as you can and then get the exercises done as required.

1. What would the most advanced, most forward-looking, most self-assured country in history do without its periodic crises of confidence? In 1957, the Soviets put a tin can into space, and the U.S. thought the sky was falling.   A   . "American decline" was all the fashion until the *vaunted* Japanese model of tight organization and industrial planning took a nosedive and a bunch of twenty-something Americans *tinkering* in their garages created untold wealth and took over the world.

2. Now, 20 years later, our newest fix of pessimism. Why? Our economic growth rate is second in the West only to tiny Finland's. It's probably just a symptom of $3 gasoline. Nonetheless, it's back. This time it's not Russia or Japan but other *inscrutable* foreigners, Indian and Chinese. What was once rather unkindly said about Brazil—"the country of the future and always will be"—I say of them. I'm not worried.

3.   B   . Mine are that the U.S. leads the world by an immense margin in just about every measure of intellectual and technological achievement: Ph.D.s, patents, peer-reviewed articles, Nobel Prizes. But in the end, it's the culture, stupid. The economy follows culture, and American culture is today, as ever, uniquely suited for growth, innovation and advancement.

> **vaunt** *v.* to boast about 吹嘘，夸耀
> **tinker** *v.* to work in a casual or inexpert way, esp trying to repair or improve sth 胡乱修理，乱改动，瞎鼓捣
> **inscrutable** *adj.* difficult to fathom or understand; impenetrable 不可思议的

20

4   The most obvious bedrock of success is entrepreneurial spirit. The U.S. has the most risk-taking, most **laissez-faire**, least regulated economy in the advanced Western world. America is heartily disdained by its coddled and controlled European cousins for its cowboy capitalism. But it is precisely America's tolerance for creative destruction—industries failing, others rising, workers changing jobs and cities and skills with an **alacrity** and **insouciance** that Europeans find astonishing—that keeps its economy **churning** and advancing.

5   Some are alarmed that government R&D funding has fallen from a 60% to a 30% share of total funding. So what? Does government necessarily make wiser investment decisions than private companies? The mistake of the Soviets, Japanese and so many others was to assume that creativity could be achieved with enough government planning and funding. ___C___. A society's creativity is directly proportionate to the rate of free interaction of people and ideas in a vast unplanned national chemical reaction. There is no country anywhere more given to the **unencumbered**, **unfettered**, unregulated exchange of ideas than the U.S.

6   ___D___. America is uniquely socially mobile, ethnically mixed and racially tolerant. America is, in Ben Wattenberg's phrase, the first universal nation, indeed the only universal nation. Every street corner in New York City is a rainbow of humanity. The resulting interaction and fusion of cultures produce not just great cuisine and music and art but also great science and technology. Intel was cofounded by a Hungarian, Google by a Russian, Yahoo! by a Chinese. We are the world's masters of **assimilation**. Where else do you see cultures and races so at home with one another?

7   Those cultural traits create the **bottom line** of our success: productivity, the closest measure of national efficiency, as well as technological creativity and ultimately wealth creation. In those areas, the U.S. continues to be the wonder of the world. From 1947 to the oil shock of 1973, our productivity grew annually at an average compounding 3% rate.

---

laissez-faire *n.* policy of freedom from government control 自由放任政策

alacrity *n.* speed or quickness; celerity 敏捷，轻快，迅速

insouciance *n.* blithe lack of concern; nonchalance 漫不经心，漠不关心

churn *v.* to move about vigorously or violently 剧烈翻腾

unencumbered *adj.* not burdened with cares or responsibilities 没有累赘的

unfettered *adj.* not limited or controlled 不受约束羁绊的

assimilation *n.* (process of) making sb become part of another social group or state 同化(的过程)

bottom line *n.phr.* (infml) deciding or crucial factor 决定性因素; essential point (in an argument, etc) (论辩的)基本论点,根本问题

For the next 20 years that rate was mysteriously cut in half, the background for much of the declinist **vogue** of the '80s. Then in the past decade, when we finally stopped playing with our **newfangled** computers and figured out how to use them, productivity returned to the magic 3% level of the immediate postwar era when America **bestrode** the world like a colossus.

8   Indeed, in the past five years, our productivity hit 3.5%, surpassing those magic years. Our only rivals at the top of the productivity list are the postage-stamp Scandinavians (Finland, Denmark and Sweden), while the **lumbering** giants we so fear, China and India, rank 49th and 50th.

> **vogue** *n.* fashion 潮流
> **newfangled** *adj.* recently designed or produced 新设计的;新创的(只作定语,多表示不赞同或不信任)
> **bestride** *v.* (fml) to sit or stand with one leg on each side of (sth) 两腿分开跨坐/站在(某物)上
> **lumber** *v.* to move in a heavy clumsy way 笨重地移动

9   True, we can ruin our future if we listen to the voices of defeatism and give in to the classic isolationist tendencies of protectionism and xenophobia. Fear could lead us to cut off trade both in goods and in brains, keeping out those wily foreigners who come here to learn our secrets and take them home. Of course, some do. They always have, but the majority are seduced by the openness, tolerance and energy of America and stay here to enrich us.

10   Our gloom amid boom is a comment more on our national mood swings than on the state of our economy or scientific culture. ___E___.

(Words: 802)

• Second Reading •

Directions: Read the text again more carefully to find enough information for Exercises I, II, III,IV & V.

Exercise I   Understanding Text Organization

Directions: You may find there are a few sentences (segments) missing from the passage. Read the article through and decide where the following sentences should go.

1. But the very essence of creativity is spontaneity.
2. And not just ideas but also the people who give life to them.
3. You can pick your statistics.
4. In the 1980s we began crying into our soup because Sony was selling so many nifty Trinitrons.
5. If we can just keep our heads, take our meds and resist fear itself, we'll do just fine.

Exercise II Multiple-Choice Questions

Directions: Please choose the best answer from the four choices given.

1. From the title, we can infer that the author _____.
   A. holds an optimistic attitude towards his country
   B. believes some people are exaggerating the fact
   C. will refute some pessimistic view at home
   D. all the above
2. The author believes that the greatest advantage of the U.S. is its _____.
   A. intellectual and technological achievement
   B. unique culture
   C. advanced economy
   D. entrepreneurial spirit
3. What is the tone of the author when he says "America is heartily disdained by its coddled and controlled European cousins for its cowboy capitalism"?
   A. Despising.   B. Admiring.   C. Mocking.   D. Indifferent.
4. The country that is at the top of the productivity list is _____.
   A. Brazil   B. Finland   C. China   D. India
5. What is NOT mentioned as a factor that can ruin the future of the U.S.?
   A. Wily foreigners.   B. Fear.
   C. Protectionism.   D. Xenophobia.

Exercise III Word Matching

Directions: Please choose the supplied words to explain the original forms of the boldfaced words in the following sentences.

A. intense dislike of foreigners   B. crafty   C. treat indulgently
D. a man of great size   E. difficult situation

1. Now, 20 years later, our newest fix of pessimism.
2. America is heartily disdained by its coddled and controlled European cousins for its cowboy capitalism.
3. …when America bestrode the world like a colossus.
4. True, we can ruin our future if we…give in to the classic isolationist tendencies of protectionism and xenophobia.
5. Fear…, keeping out those wily foreigners who come here to learn our secrets and take them home.

Exercise IV   Short-Answer Questions

Directions: Please answer the following questions briefly in your own words.

1. How do you understand the sentence "But in the end, it's the culture, stupid"?
2. What cultural traits of the U.S. are emphasized as unique?
3. What elements make the bottom line of the success of America?

Exercise V   Discussion

Directions: Please discuss the following questions in pairs or groups.

1. What should we do to enhance our competitiveness in the world?
2. How do you deal with xenophobia if you go abroad?

Text C

Supreme Court Rejects School Racial Diversity Plans

By Warren Richey

1   While the race of a student can be one of many characteristics taken into consideration to achieve diversity in the student body, it may not become the predominant criterion that determines which students are admitted to the most popular schools in a district.

2   In a major 5-to-4 decision announced Thursday, the US Supreme Court struck down race-based public school enrollment plans in Seattle and Louisville, Ky., that were designed to maintain racially integrated student populations. The majority justices said the plans were unconstitutional because they relied too heavily on race in violation of the mandate that all Americans be treated equally regardless of skin color or ethnicity.

3   "What do the racial classifications at issue here do, if not accord differential treatment on the basis of race?" asks Chief Justice John Roberts in his majority opinion.

4   In announcing the ruling, Chief Justice Roberts gave public-school administrators throughout the nation perhaps their toughest assignment yet: Find a way to remain faithful to the promise of racially integrated schools under the landmark 1954 decision, Brown v. Board of Education, but do it without paying inordinate attention to the racial or ethnic background of the students.

5   The decision in two consolidated cases is likely to spark legal challenges to many affirmative-action plans and other proactive race-conscious measures aimed at reaching out to African-Americans and other minorities.

6   The ruling brought immediate and heated reaction.

7   "We're very outraged by it, and we'll fight it, as we say, by any means necessary," says George Washington, a lawyer with the Coalition to Defend Affirmative Action in Detroit. "It's an attempt to end racial progress in this country. It's an attempt to freeze de facto segregation as it now exists in this country."

8   Others praised the opinion. "School boards will look at this decision and see that Seattle and Louisville failed," says Roger Clegg, president of the Center for Equal Opportunity in Falls Church, Va. "That, plus the fact that I think racial and ethnic preferences are increasingly unpopular with students and parents of all races will persuade most schools not to engage in this kind of discrimination."

9   The 41-page decision backs away from some of the constitutional ground staked out four years ago in June 2003, when then Justice Sandra Day O'Connor cast the deciding vote in a 5-to-4 decision upholding the use of race to achieve student diversity at the prestigious University of Michigan Law School.

10   Justice Anthony Kennedy wrote a dissent in that case accusing the majority justices in the Michigan Law School decision of abandoning the high constitutional bar that had traditionally been applied by the court to the use of race in the context of university admissions. Thursday's decision beefs up that constitutional scrutiny, but Justice Kennedy declined to join the court's four conservatives in adopting a colorblind approach in matters of school enrollment. Such an approach would have potentially closed the door on all race-based plans.

11   School officials have a compelling interest in avoiding racial isolation and in achieving a diverse student population, Kennedy writes in a concurring opinion. "Race may be one component of that diversity, but other demographic factors, plus special talents and needs, should also be considered," he says.

12   As in the high court's April 18 abortion decision, the shift in its race-based enrollment jurisprudence can be linked to Justice O'Connor's retirement from the court and her replacement by a more conservative justice, Samuel Alito.

13   Both sides of the sharply divided court attempted to wrap their arguments in references to Brown v. Board of Education.

14   In his majority opinion, the chief justice quoted from a second Brown decision in 1955 as requiring government officials "to achieve a system of determining admission to the public schools *on a nonracial basis*."

15   "What do racial classifications do in these cases, if not determine admissions to a public school on a racial basis?" Roberts asks.

16   "Before Brown, schoolchildren were told where they could and could not go to school based on the color of their skin," he writes. "The school districts in these cases have not carried the heavy burden of demonstrating that we should allow this once again—even for very different reasons."

17   In a 68-page dissent, Justice Stephen Breyer said that to invalidate the Seattle and Louisville enrollment plans "is to threaten the promise of Brown."

18   "What was the hope and promise of Brown?" Justice Breyer asks. "It was the promise of true racial equality—not as a matter of fine words on paper, but as a matter of everyday life in the nation's cities and schools."

19   Breyer warns that the majority's position will undercut the larger significance of Brown. "This is a decision that the court and the nation will come to regret," he writes.

20   Both of the challenged enrollment plans in Louisville and Seattle attempted to address de facto segregation tied in part to housing patterns. The voluntary desegregation programs were aimed at preventing the school districts from sliding into a starkly segregated environment with minority students isolated in inner-city schools and white students isolated in suburban

schools.

21   To achieve a meaningful mix, school boards in Louisville and Seattle decided that they would sometimes have to use race as a factor to determine which students could attend the most popular schools.

22   In Seattle, the school board set enrollment at the district's most desired high schools within 15 percentage points of the overall racial balance of the district's students. The balance was 40 percent white and 60 percent nonwhite.

23   Students were permitted to attend any of the district's 10 high schools. But because some schools were more popular than others, the board created a racial tiebreaker to determine eligibility to attend the most popular schools.

24   If a new student would cause that particular school's white or nonwhite student population to increase above the 55 percent cutoff, the student was barred from attending that school.

25   Opponents of the plan said Seattle schools were already diverse and that the race tiebreaker was a form of unconstitutional racial balancing.

26   Lawyers for the school board argued that integration efforts are not the same as racial discrimination. There is a fundamental difference between using race to segregate students and using it to integrate them, they said.

27   In Louisville, the Jefferson County School Board established a broad goal that each of the district's schools should have black student enrollment set between 15 percent and 50 percent of the school's total enrollment. African-American enrollment districtwide is about 35 percent. School administrators set the exact racial mix at each school.

28   The program tries to encourage students to attend schools outside their neighborhood to help achieve meaningful diversity in every school in the district. School officials urge parents to be flexible in considering an array of second-and third-choice schools to avoid disappointment over being denied admission to a single favored school for racial reasons.

29   Parents opposed to the plan say it denies a government benefit based on skin color. Supporters say all schools in the district are essentially the same in offering a public education, so being admitted to one school instead of another does not amount to a benefit.

30   The two cases decided Thursday are Parents Involved in Community Schools v. Seattle School District No. 1 (05-908) and Crystal Meredith v. Jefferson County Board of Education (05-915). Complete decisions and dissents are available on the Supreme Court's website at www.supremecourtus.gov/index.html.

(Words: 1280)

Exercise I Discussion

Directions: Please discuss the following questions in pairs or groups.

1. Why is racial diversity considered so important in US schools? And why is it said that the Supreme Court's new ruling "gave public-school administrators throughout the nation perhaps their toughest assignment yet"?
2. What do you know about Brown v. Board of Education? Why did both sides of the sharply divided court attempt to wrap their arguments in references to it?
3. Which side will you support? Why?

Exercise II Writing

Directions: Write a composition in around 150 words either about your own opinions on one of the controversial issues discussed in the texts or about the future prospects of the United States in the fast-changing world.

UNIT THREE

COLLEGE AND RESPONSIBILITY

*T*arget of the Unit

☞ To learn about some challenges facing colleges and their students and what ways universities and society are taking to tackle the problems
☞ To practice reading skills
☞ To enlarge your vocabulary

1) LEAD IN

Directions: In this unit, you will read 3 passages about different aspects of the responsibilities colleges and universities should take. Read them with a critical eye and think about what social responsibility college students in China should take.

2) DISCUSSION

What roles should a college or university play in the cultivation of a person? What is its role in the development of society? And how about the responsibility of college students?

Text A

What Exactly Does GW's President Do?

By Stephen Joel Trachtenberg

*W*arming-up Exercises

☞ In your opinion, what does a university president do?
☞ Who is an ideal university president in your eyes?

First reading

Directions: Now please read the following passage as fast as you can and summarize the main idea.

1 The student, an undergraduate, had a problem. She was getting ready to enroll in GW's upcoming semester, but had no place to live for a couple of days before the semester actually began.

2 So my wife and I invited her to stay with our family, and over dinner on the first evening of her visit she said to me, "Excuse me for asking, but what exactly does a university president *do*?"

3 My initial reaction, as I hardly need to tell you, was one of hurt. Wasn't it *obvious* that I was performing my duties in what amounted to a six-day week and a sixteen-hour day, and dealing with countless emergencies in the process—a few of which could actually threaten the future of the University?

4 Then, I tried saying to myself: "maybe it's not so obvious from an 'outside' point of view how a university president like you actually spends average time on an average day."

5 So I got ready to write my article for *The Hatchet*, and I started out by making a list:

6 Duties of GW's President:

7 *Balance and harmonize the various "turfs" represented by GW's Vice-Presidents.* Sounds good, doesn't it? But sometimes it requires a lot of political skill and even more political determination.

8 *Worry about money.* It's exhilarating to be in charge of a school that's on an upward climb at the pace of GW. But as you might expect if you're a university located in Foggy Bottom, brilliant and innovative ideas often cost a lot as they turn into classrooms, laboratories and studios—all staffed by faculty members whose salaries are competitive with those being offered by other top schools.

9 Parents and families don't like to hear that their son or daughter is going to a school run by the banks to which it owes a fortune.

10 *Keep a sharp eye on the media, and on how they are reporting on and/or affecting GW faculty, students and alumni.* The fashionable reaction is, "Oh! You mean that today's university president is nothing but a public relations person." This response, I must confess, always makes

my blood run very cold. And if I said what was really in my heart, it would run as follows, "That's just an insufferably **snobbish** and conceited way of saying that this University is in a continuous state of public exposure."

11 Somebody has to keep a vigilant eye on a reality that huge, especially when it is a reality that decides this University's present and future.

> **snobbish** *adj.* of, befitting, or resembling a snob; pretentious 势利眼的
> **powerhouse** *n.* (fig) very powerful group, organization, etc (比喻)强大的组织、团体等; a highly energetic and indefatigable person 干将
> **bump into** *v.phr.* to meet by chance 偶遇
> **telephonically** *adv.* by telephonic means or processes; by the use of the telephone 通过使用电话
> **symphony** *n.* a consonance or harmony of sounds, agreeable to the ear, whether the sounds are vocal or instrumental, or both 交响（乐）

12 *Never miss an opportunity to project the University's image, so laden with academic virtue, in ways that confirm that image's essential accuracy.* Somebody has to coordinate the look and feel of an academic institution that mails out literally millions of pieces of paper each year. And somebody has to serve as the ultimate spokesperson for GW when the media call—which they increasingly do.

13 *Feel comfortable in conversation with everyone from the President of the United States to foreign heads of state.* When a school is engaged in a "boom" as vigorous as the one that now typifies GW, national and international involvements swiftly multiply. In recent years, I have found myself in intense personal conversation with the chief officials of New Zealand, Morocco, Israel, Costa Rica, Egypt and other nations. All were people who thought of GW as an intellectual and pedagogical **powerhouse**. So I had to look and sound like a university president whose daily climb into the cabin of his powerhouse was something he took for granted!

14 *Keep in touch, at a plausible, personal level, with all of the constituencies represented by the University.* The young woman of my first paragraph, who needed temporary housing, was someone I ran into on a food line at our J Street cafeteria. Across the desk from me I see faculty members on countless occasions. Informal personal conversations number hundreds in an average year. Staff I "**bump into**" wherever I go on this campus, either personally or **telephonically**.

15 So I'm actually a "sad musician" of sorts, racing around one of the biggest concerts on our planet, urging the trumpets to play a little louder or the second violinist to stop sneering at the first. The result is a **symphony** notable for its harmonics rather than for grunts, groans, screams of pain, and missed opportunities. GW is the kind of a place that feels proudest when it delivers exactly the services it markets to the public—above all, the capacity to earn one's living, after graduation, in ways that fill the soul while they also fill the wallet and the stomach.

16   GW's success is synonymous with the success of its students and faculty. And that, in turn, is just one of the reasons that a university president like me runs so energetically from place to place and subject to subject, trying to make things even better!

(Words: 824)

Second Reading

Directions: Read the text again more carefully to find enough information for Exercises I, II & III.

Exercise I   True or False

Directions: Please state whether the following statements are true or not (T/F) according to the text.

1. The author used to believe that others know what he does on an average day.
2. The author writes this article for the undergraduate student.
3. GW's President is constantly confronted with some problems that threaten the future of the university.
4. As GW's President, it is hard to deal with its Vice-Presidents.
5. Parents usually don't care whether the school their children are attending is wealthy or not.
6. In the author's opinion, the media will always decide the university's present and future.
7. GW's President should also work as the spokesman of the university.
8. GW's President should keep in touch with the staff.
9. GW's President should try to make everybody in the university satisfied with the school.
10. GW's President projects the future of the students to be wealthy both spiritually and materially.

Exercise II   Word Inference

Directions: Often you can guess the meaning of a word/expression by reading the words around it. Please read the given sentence to see how each word/expression in bold type is used in the text. Then choose the answer that is closest in meaning to the bold-faced word/expression.

1. Balance and harmonize the various "**turfs**" represented by GW's Vice-Presidents.
   A. one's own area   B. bureaucracy   C. party   D. track
2. It's **exhilarating** to be in charge of a school that's on an upward climb at the pace of GW.
   A. exciting   B. ordinary   C. of sb's duty   D. hard
3. This response, I must **confess**, always makes my blood run very cold.
   A. say   B. feel   C. admit   D. be happy
4. That's just an insufferably snobbish and **conceited** way of saying that this University is in a continuous state of public exposure.
   A. clever   B. easy
   C. better   D. excessively proud
5. Somebody has to keep a **vigilant** eye on a reality that huge, especially when it is a reality that decides this University's present and future.
   A. vigorous   B. secret   C. sharp   D. busy
6. Never miss an opportunity to project the University's image, so **laden** with academic virtue, in ways that confirm that image's essential accuracy.
   A. famous   B. proud   C. filled   D. care
7. All were people who thought of GW as an intellectual and **pedagogical** powerhouse.
   A. relating to the study of intellects
   B. relating to the practice of teaching
   C. relating to the study of people
   D. relating to the practice of administrating
8. Keep in touch, at a **plausible**, personal level, with all of the constituencies represented by the University.
   A. reasonable   B. personal   C. high   D. frequent
9. The result is a symphony notable for its **harmonics** rather than for grunts, groans, screams of pain, and missed opportunities.
   A. harmony
   B. pleasant atmosphere
   C. happy mood
   D. the way notes are played or sung together to give a pleasing sound
10. GW's success is **synonymous** with the success of its students and faculty.
    A. having the same meaning
    B. having the opposite meaning
    C. keeping up
    D. going together

Exercise III   Discussion

Directions: Please discuss the following questions in pairs or groups.

1. Do you think a university president should also be a scholar or only an administrator?
2. In addition to the duties mentioned in the text, what else should a university president do?

Text B

Campuses Slow to Deal with Growth in Gambling

By Matt Bradley

Warming-up Exercises

☞ Do you think gambling is also a problem for Chinese college students? If yes, what do you think the college should do to deal with the problem?

☞ What forms of gambling are now rampaging university campuses in China?

First reading

Directions: Now please read the following passage as fast as you can and summarize the main idea.

1   When a local **bookie** demanded that Jay either pay up or take a beating, the University of Maryland student might have realized he had a gambling problem.

2   "I did actually go to Gamblers' Anonymous," says Jay, now 28, who asked that his last name not be used. "At that time, it was hard because I was a college student, and I couldn't relate to the problems [adult gamblers] were having with their families and wives.... I didn't stay because it didn't make sense to me. I just thought I was a college kid trying to have fun."

3   Amid the wide range of

> **bookie** *n.* someone whose job is to collect money that people want to risk on the result of a race, competition etc, and who pays them if they guess correctly 赌注登记经纪人

drug, alcohol, and rape-crisis counseling programs at his school, Jay found little help for his gambling problem, despite what he saw as an **endemic** betting culture on campus.

4   These days, the "hobby" formerly known as a vice is more glamorous than ever. College students are the prize **demographic** for arresting cable-TV poker competitions and glittery betting websites.

They came, they had fun, and they learned about the odds of winning during Casino Day. Shown (top left) are Viral Narsinh of Fort Smith, Souk Chaleunsack of Van Buren, Brandon Vick of Van Buren, Arron Kimes of Booneville, and Prakash Padhiar of Fort Smith. Kayla Taylor of Barling (right) calls numbers in bingo, and Wesley Travis of Fort Smith (bottom left) plots his strategies.

5   ___A___. But pitched against a student body flush with easy credit, Internet access, and idle time, gambling's lure may have the better hand.

6   Among young American men ages 14 to 22, the number who said they gambled once a month rose by 20 percent from 2004 to 2005, according to the Annenberg Public Policy Center at the University of Pennsylvania. Of the 2.9 million young people who gamble every week, 80 percent are men.

7   "At the college and university level, poker is pretty much the hottest thing going," says Mike Edwards, business development and marketing manager for absolutepoker.com.   ___B___.

8   "We want to embrace this, and we want to create a unique value proposition for students who are playing poker online," Mr. Edwards said by phone. The company is based in Canada, where gambling is legal. Online gambling is now a $12 billion industry, up from $3.1 billion in 2001, according to industry analyst, Christiansen Capital Advisors, with the majority of Internet casinos operating outside the US.

9   "In our view, much of the media **glamorization** of gambling has been done without any responsible gaming message," says Keith Whyte, executive director of the National Council on Problem Gambling in Washington, D.C. "Can you imagine a world series of drinking?" he says, alluding to the televised "World Series of Poker." "It would have warning signs and responsible consumption messages. You see almost none of that with televised gambling shows."

endemic *adj.* an endemic disease or problem is always present in a particular place, or among a particular group of people 地方性的，某一人群所特有的
demographic *n.* a part of the population that is considered as a group, especially by advertisers who want to sell things to that group 特定人群
glamorization *n.* the act of glamorizing; making sth or someone more beautiful (often in a superficial way) 美化

10   One recent, though extreme, example of the problems gambling has created for college students involved Greg Hogan, the sophomore class president at Lehigh University, who last month robbed a bank in Allentown, Pa. Mr. Hogan had run up about $5,000 in Internet

gambling debts.

11   The private nature and deep penetrations of Internet gambling has rendered nearly unenforceable any rules designed to **curb** the campus betting culture. ___C___.

12   "The vast majority of schools we talk to have no formal or informal policy regarding [gambling]," says Mr. Whyte. "They see gambling as almost a victimless crime. That's certainly the way it's treated by law enforcement. In general, there's a lack of awareness."

13   Extending the same counseling services to problem gamblers that are normally afforded to alcoholics and drug abusers, however, is a different story. Jeffrey Derevensky, codirector for the International Center for Youth Gambling Problems & High Risk Behaviour at McGill University in Montreal, says many campuses are behind when it comes to counseling strategies needed to meet gambling addictions.

14   "I don't think they can regulate it, but I think they should provide counseling services and be aware that this is a problem," says Mr. Derevensky. "Most counselors have very little training in terms of understanding what the issues are around gambling and what constitutes a gambling problem."

> **curb** *v.* to check, restrain, or control as if with a curb; rein in 遏制, 阻止
> **addiction-prone** *adj.* addiction: compulsive physiological and psychological need for a habit-forming substance 成瘾, 嗜好; prone: having a tendency or inclination, being likely 容易, 易成为; 合起来的意思就是"容易上瘾"
> **exacerbate** *v.* to make a bad situation worse 加剧, 恶化

15   ___D___. The new programming strategy aims first to address the lack of awareness among parents, staff, and students. Kim Dude, director of Missouri's Wellness Resource Center, anticipates playing a pioneering role.

16   "I'm excited about the fact that it's cutting edge," says Ms. Dude. "I wish there were other resources to tap into, but since there aren't, we're going to create resources for other campuses."

17   Experts recommend prevention strategies similar to those used with drugs and alcohol—namely, youth education. As with smoking, drinking, and illegal drug use, the earlier someone starts gambling, the more **addiction-prone** they become, says the National Research Council, a nonprofit policy think tank in Washington, D.C. A high school gambling habit can be **exacerbated** in an unsupervised college environment, says Whyte. ___E___.

18   "If you're not reaching kids by middle school, by the time [they] get to college, we can't do prevention campaigns anymore," says Whyte. "Most college kids have gambled. It's all about education."

19   But until antigambling education is the norm in grade school, the fact that gambling appears to have taken off with the "beautiful people" won't help.

(Words:819)

• Second Reading •

Directions: Read the text again more carefully to find enough information for Exercises I, II, III,IV & V.

Exercise I Understanding Text Organization

Directions: You may find there are a few sentences (segments) missing from the passage. Read the article through and decide where the following sentences should go.

1. Tackling problem gamblers before college students leave home—or enter high school—is a crucial preventive strategy.
2. The prevailing social attitudes and typically permissive campus climates may also contribute to the lack of action.
3. University administrators may finally be looking to address the trend.
4. One of the first counseling efforts to treat problem gambling is in its infancy at the University of Missouri-Columbia.
5. The Internet poker website caters to college students by offering to pay a semester's tuition for tournament winners.

Exercise II Multiple-Choice Questions

Directions: Please choose the best answer from the four choices given.

1. In the case of Jay, what did he get from his school?
   A. He got financial support from gamble-crisis counseling program.
   B. He got mental help from gamble-crisis counseling program.
   C. He got mental help from drug-crisis counseling program.
   D. He got little help.
2. What is the most popular game at the college and university level?
   A. Poker.   B. Internet gambling.
   C. Roulette.   D. Casino.
3. Why is the Internet poker website so frequently visited by college students?
   A. Because students can have a lot of fun.
   B. Because students can play with their friends.
   C. Because students can make friends there.

D. Because students can get a semester's tuition if they win.

4. What's the problem with televised gambling shows according to Keith Whyte?

    A. They encourage young people to gamble.

    B. They do not have any warning signs.

    C. They are too often shown on mass media.

    D. They try to operate within the US.

5. Why is it difficult to extend counseling services to problem gamblers on campus?

    A. Because most students are reluctant to seek help from the service.

    B. Because most counselors have little training in dealing with the gambling issue.

    C. Because most counselors see no necessity to offer the service.

    D. Because parents do not want to pay for the service.

Exercise III   Word Matching

Directions: Please choose the supplied words to explain the original forms of the boldfaced words in the following sentences.

A. forefront   B. habitual heavy drinker
C. refer indirectly   D. expect   E. have plenty of

1. But pitched against a student body **flush** with easy credit, Internet access, and idle time, gambling's lure may have the better hand.

2. "Can you imagine a world series of drinking?" he says, **alluding to** the televised "World Series of Poker."

3. "I'm excited about the fact that it's **cutting edge**," says Ms. Dude.

4. Extending the same counseling services to problem gamblers that are normally afforded to **alcoholics** and drug abusers, however, is a different story.

5. The new programming strategy aims first to address the lack of awareness among parents, staff, and students. Kim Dude, director of Missouri's Wellness Resource Center, **anticipates** playing a pioneering role.

Exercise IV   Short-Answer Questions

Directions: Please answer the following questions briefly in your own words.

1. Why does Kim Dude, director of Missouri's Wellness Resource Center, believe their efforts will play a pioneering role?

2. Why do we need to start with middle school students to prevent problem gambling?
3. What are the things colleges and universities should do to curb campus gambling according to the passage?

Exercise V Discussion

Directions: Please discuss the following questions in pairs or groups.

1. What are the causes for the prevailing of school gambling culture?
2. Do you think counseling services on campus are important for students? Why?

Text C

Gates Urges Graduates to Tackle Global Inequity

By Alvin Powell

1   Microsoft founder Bill Gates returned to Harvard Thursday (June 7) to finally collect his degree—an honorary doctorate—and to urge the Class of 2007 to change the world for the millions who live in poverty and die of preventable diseases each year.

2   The world's problems may seem intractable, Gates said, but with the advances in technology and the resources at the disposal of today's graduates, they have never been more solvable.

3   Gates quoted his mother, saying, "From those to whom much is given, much is expected," and added that the world has enormous expectations of those from Harvard.

4   "When you consider what those of us here in this Yard have been given—in talent, privilege, and opportunity—there is almost no limit to what the world has a right to expect from us," Gates said. "Be activists. Take on the big inequities. It will be one of the great experiences of your lives."

5   Gates was the Commencement Day speaker during the annual meeting of the Harvard Alumni Association in Harvard's

Tercentenary Theatre. Commencement exercises at Harvard consist of two main parts. Degrees are conferred on the year's graduates during Morning Exercises in Tercentenary Theatre, the area between the Memorial Church and Widener Library. This year, more than 6,000 graduates of Harvard College and Harvard's graduate schools joined the ranks of 330,000 alumni in 185 countries around the world, according to Alumni Association President Paul J. Finnegan.

6 The Afternoon Exercises consist of the annual meeting of the Harvard Alumni Association, which included both the day's graduates and alumni from years past. It is during the annual meeting of the Harvard Alumni Association that the Commencement speaker delivers his or her address.

7 Harvard interim President Derek Bok also addressed the afternoon assembly. Just weeks before his successor, Drew G. Faust, takes office on July 1, Bok presented what he sees as challenges facing higher education generally and Harvard specifically.

8 Like Gates, Bok sees opportunity facing today's Harvard. Bok said that in today's information age the University—and other universities around the world—play more important roles than ever. Demand for the services of higher education is growing, he said, and therein lies the challenge. How do universities meet that demand? Who do they educate and how? How do they measure and improve that education? And, with the knowledge generated at universities at a premium, what services beyond education—such as consulting for government and market reform—should they provide?

9 Bok said enormous opportunities lie in the sciences, with technology fueling discoveries in genomics, neuroscience, and a host of other areas. Universities of the future will have to decide how best to take advantage of the scientific opportunities that present themselves.

10 In addition, Bok said, universities have to figure out how to encourage robust growth in the humanities. While some may think there's a danger that the humanities will wither in the shadow of science's growth, Bok said the societal and cultural changes and the ethical dilemmas posed by scientific advances can only be answered by the humanities.

11 "The traditional focus of the humanities on questions of value, meaning, ethics are more important than ever before," Bok said. "Far from marginalizing the humanities, universities must look for ways to encourage humanists to address such questions in ways we can all understand so they can help us build a world where our scientific advances don't overwhelm us, but are made to serve humane purposes," he said.

12 Bok said one must look back to the period after the Civil War to find a time of such opportunity for Harvard.

13 "This is a much more formidable agenda than I have seen in my lifetime. It is also more significant," Bok said. "Universities matter more to society today than ever before. Harvard

is especially important, since we now possess the greatest collection of exceptional students, talented faculty, and financial resources of any university on Earth. Deciding how to use those remarkable talents for the greatest good is an awesome responsibility of vital interest to everyone."

14 Gates, who spoke after Bok, reflected on his own Harvard experience. Though he dropped out to start Microsoft, Gates said Harvard was a "phenomenal experience" for him. The knowledge he gained and the people he met at Harvard proved immensely important in his life.

15 "It could be exhilarating, intimidating, sometimes even discouraging, but always challenging," Gates said. "It was an amazing privilege—and though I left early, I was transformed by my years at Harvard, the friendships I made, and the ideas I worked on."

16 Gates said one thing he did not learn at Harvard, however, was about the world's inequities. He said he was shocked to learn that millions of children die each year of diseases that are absent from the industrialized world and that could be treated if the will was there.

17 After analyzing the problem, Gates said, he figured out the cruel reason that nothing had been done.

18 "The answer is simple and hard. The market did not reward saving the lives of these children, and governments did not subsidize it. So the children died because their mothers and fathers had no power in the market and no voice in the system," Gates said. "But you and I have both."

19 Gates urged graduates and others in the audience to work to create market forces that provide incentives—profits for businesses and votes for politicians—to help the world's poorest and least fortunate.

20 Gates said he believes that the biggest barrier to solving the problems of inequity is not a lack of caring, as some believe, but that finding ways to contribute are too complex. Many people, he said, would help if they only knew how.

21 To do that, he said, requires determining a goal, finding the highest-impact approach, discovering the ideal technology for that approach, and continuing to do what works best now while those other things are going on. And above all, he said, don't get discouraged.

22 "The crucial thing is to never stop thinking and working—and never do what we did with malaria and tuberculosis in the 20th century—which was to surrender to complexity and quit," Gates said. "In line with the promise of this age, I want to exhort each of the graduates here to take on an issue—a complex problem, a deep inequity, and become a specialist on it…. You have more than we had. You must start sooner and carry on longer."

(Words: 1094)

Exercise I Discussion

Directions: Please discuss the following questions in pairs or groups.

1. What are the functions of a modern university?
2. In today's information age, how do universities meet the demand of society?
3. What is the balance between science and humanities? Why are the humanities especially important in the era of rapid development of science?

Exercise II Writing

Directions: Suppose you become a celebrity after graduation and you're invited back to your university to give a speech to the students. Try to write what you want to say to them in about 150 words.

UNIT FOUR

"NEW" GENERATIONS

Target of the Unit

☞ To learn about some facts and conflicts concerning different generations in the U.S.
☞ To practice reading skills
☞ To enlarge your vocabulary

1) LEAD IN

Directions: In this unit, you will read 3 passages depicting the life of different generations in the contemporary world, especially those of the western countries. Try to compare the differing values and demands of these generations, and notice the new features they exhibit in this age of rapid changes.

2) DISCUSSION

What do you know about the generation division in the U.S. since WW II?

Text A

What Gen Y Really Wants

By Penelope Trunk

Warming-up Exercises

☞ What are the differences between the elderly people in their fifties or sixties and the young people in their twenties?
☞ In your opinion, how can we achieve a work-life balance?

First reading

Directions: Now please read the following passage as fast as you can and summarize the main idea.

1   With 85 million **baby boomers** and 50 million Gen Xers, there is already a yawning generation gap among American workers—particularly in their ideas of work-life balance. For baby boomers, it's the juggling act between job and family. For Gen X, it means moving in and out of the workforce to accommodate kids and outside interests. Now along come the 76 million members of Generation Y. For these new 20-something workers, the line between work and home doesn't really exist. They just want to spend their time in meaningful and useful ways, no matter where they are.

2   The first challenge for the companies that want to hire the best young workers is getting them in the door. They are in high demand—the baby boomers are retiring, and many Gen X workers are opting out of long hours—and they have high expectations for personal growth, even in **entry-level jobs**. More than half of Generation Y's new graduates move back to their parents' homes after collecting their degrees, and that cushion of support gives them the time to pick the job they really want. Taking time off to travel used to be **a résumé red flag**; today it's a learning experience. And entrepreneurship now functions as a safety net for this generation. They grew up on the Internet, and they know how to launch a viable online business. Facebook, for example, began in a college dorm room.

3   With all these options, Generation Y is forcing companies to think more creatively about work-life balance. The employers who do are winning in the war for young talent. The consulting firm Deloitte was alarmed by the high turnover of its youngest employees, so it asked one of its consultants, Stan Smith, to find out more about what attracts them to and keeps them at a job. His research reveals that job hopping is not an end in itself but something young workers do when they see no other choice.

4   "People would rather stay at one company and grow, but they don't think they can do that," he says. "Two-thirds of the people

> **baby boomer** *n.phr.* It is a term used to describe a person who was born during the Post-World War II baby boom between 1946 and 1964. Following World War II, several English-speaking countries—the United States, Canada, Australia, and New Zealand—experienced an unusual spike in birth rates, a phenomenon commonly referred to as the baby boom. 婴儿潮年代出生的孩子
>
> **entry-level job** *n.phr.* a job appropriate for or accessible to one who is inexperienced in a field or new to a market 入门水平工作，低级别工作
>
> **red flag** *n.* (Am.) something that shows or warms you that something might be wrong, illegal etc. 警示信号，危险信号

who left Deloitte left to do something they could have done with us, but we made it difficult for them to transition." So Smith, who is now in charge of recruiting and retaining Generation Y as national director of next-generation initiatives, created programs at Deloitte that focus on helping people figure out their next career move. Smith is betting that in many cases, the best place for a restless young person is simply another spot in Deloitte. This saves the company the $150,000 cost of losing an employee—not to mention the stress for employees of changing jobs.

5　　Old assumptions about what employees value in the workplace don't always apply with Gen Y. Friendship is such a strong motivator for them that Gen Y workers will choose a job just to be with their friends. Boston-based Gentle Giant Moving once hired an entire athletic team. "It looked like a great work environment because of the people," says rower Niles Kuronen, 26. "It was huge to be able to work with friends." It feels normal for Gen Y employees to check in by **BlackBerry** all weekend as long as they have flexibility during the week. Sun Microsystem's telecommuting program, for example, has kicked into high gear in response to Generation Y's demands. Today more than half of Sun's employees work remotely.

> **BlackBerry** *n.* The BlackBerry solution consists of smartphones integrated with software that enables access to email and other communication services. 黑莓手机

6　　Generation Y's search for meaning makes support for volunteering among the benefits it values most. More than half of workers in their 20s prefer employment at companies that provide volunteer opportunities, according to a recent Deloitte survey. The software company Salesforce.com gives 1% of profits to its foundation, which pays for employees to volunteer 1% of their work time. Salesforce.com staff will do 50,000 hours of community service this year. "This program has dramatically increased our ability to recruit and retain high-quality employees," says CEO Marc Benioff. It's what attracted Eliot Moore, 26. "When I heard about the Salesforce.com Foundation, it was plus after plus for me," he says. "It's a way to take the skills I learned in the corporate arena and give back to the community without leaving the company."

7　　Understanding Generation Y is important not just for employers. Older workers—that is, anyone over 30—need to know how to adapt to the values and demands of their newest colleagues. Before too long, they'll be the bosses.

(Words: 739)

• Second Reading •

Directions: Read the text again more carefully to find enough information for Exercises I, II & III.

Exercise I   True or False

Directions: Please state whether the following statements are true or not (T/F) according to the text.

1. There is not much discrepancy between baby boomers and Gen Xers.
2. For Gen Ys, workers in their 20s, there is not a clear division between work and home.
3. Gen Ys are in high demand only because Gen Xs don't want to work overtime.
4. More than half of Generation Y's new graduates move back to their parents' homes after collecting their degrees because they can get support from parents.
5. Taking time off to travel used to be appreciated by your boss.
6. Companies actually have to think more creatively about the work-life balance for Gen Y.
7. Stan Smith found out that job hopping is not an end in itself but something young workers do when they see another choice.
8. Friendship is very important for Gen Y workers in choosing a job.
9. Sun Microsystem's telecommuting program, for example, has responds well to Generation Y's demands.
10. Less than half of workers in their 20s prefer employment at companies that provide volunteer opportunities.

Exercise II   Word Inference

Directions: Often you can guess the meaning of a word/expression by reading the words around it. Please read the given sentence to see how each word/expression in bold type is used in the text. Then choose the answer that is closest in meaning to the bold-faced word/expression.

1. There are 85 million baby boomers and 50 million Gen Xers, there is already a **yawning** generation gap among American workers.
   A. gaping   B. yawnful   C. drowsy   D. large

2. It's the **juggling** act between job and family.
   A. struggling   B. jugging
   C. jogging   D. coping with two or more things
3. It means moving in and out of the workforce to **accommodate** kids and outside interests.
   A. range   B. hold
   C. consider   D. take care of
4. Gen X workers are **opting out of** long hours.
   A. preferring   B. getting out of
   C. choosing not to do   D. getting rid of
5. … and that **cushion** of support gives them the time to pick the job they really want.
   A. buffer   B. padding   C. shock   D. cousin
6. They grew up on the Internet, and they know how to launch a **viable** online business.
   A. favorable   B. practicable C. liable   D. newborn
7. The consulting firm Deloitte was alarmed by the high **turnover** of its youngest employees, …
   A. overthrow   B. upset
   C. job-changing rate   D. makeover
8. So Smith, who is now in charge of recruiting and **retaining** Generation Y as national director of next-generation initiatives, …
   A. maintaining   B. keeping
   C. firing   D. hiring
9. Smith is betting that in many cases, the best place for a **restless** young person is simply another spot in Deloitte.
   A. excited   B. troubled   C. anxious   D. vigorous
10. Friendship is such a strong **motivator** for them that Gen Y workers will choose a job just to be with their friends.
    A. motion   B. purpose   C. reason   D. inducement

Exercise III Discussion

Directions: Please discuss the following questions in pairs or groups.

1. In Paragraph 2, the author argues that taking time off to travel used to be a résumé red flag, while today it's a learning experience. How do you understand it?
2. In your opinion, what are the major traits of the Gen Ys?

Text B

What Will You Call Me When I'm 64?

By Jack Rosenthal

Warming-up Exercises

☞ What euphemisms do you often use to address elderly people on given occasions?
☞ Why must we use euphemisms in our daily interactions with people?

• First reading •

Directions: Now please read the following passage as fast as you can and summarize the main idea.

1   If Shakespeare were still alive, he would be 443 this year and would recognize the need to revise one of his most famous passages, the Seven Ages of Man. Infant, schoolboy, lover, soldier, justice, shrunk shank and then second childishness—these fall well short of describing our new age of age.

2   ___A___. Hence the Shakespearean problem: What to call these millions.

3   Harry (Rick) Moody, a scholar on the subject of aging, describes the great majority as the *wellderly*, distinct from the afflicted *illderly*. But that witty distinction doesn't solve the larger nomenclature problem. ___B___.

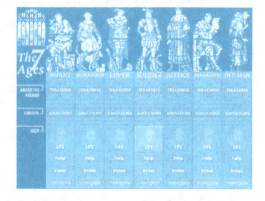

4   No variation of *elderly* **encompasses** the vast variety and abilities of people over 55 or 65. Yet we keep looking for a single **generic** term. ___C___. Then there are outright coarse insults like *geezers, gaffers, crocks* or

wellderly *n.* America's healthy elderly people are known as the wellderly—those 80 years and older with no history of chronic disease 健康老人
illderly *n.* those for whom health is the main focus of their lives 终生疾病缠身者
encompass *v.* to constitute or include 包含
generic *adj.* relating to or descriptive of an entire group or class; general 类的; 通用的, 普遍的

48

gomers, the acronym that some cranky doctors use to mean "get out of my emergency room."

5 __D__. *Boomers*, describing those born when the population started to bulge in 1946, are only now starting to enter their 60s. *Retirees* is an imperfect generalization because, for one thing, many people retire young and, for another, many older people continue to work, whether for the money or the satisfaction.

6 I've now learned from personal experience that even once-neutral terms have become troublesome. I'm involved with a new organization called ReServe that connects skilled people, near or at retirement age, with part-time jobs at nonprofit agencies in New York City. What to call them? They bridle even at inoffensive standbys like *elders* and *older adults*. An earlier generation found *senior citizens* acceptable; and *senior* as an adjective, as in *senior vice president*, remains so. But not as a noun, as in *seniors*.

7 Why? Not out of denial or vanity but because the experience of older people shows that any such generalization ignites unthinking discrimination—what Dr. Robert Butler, the longevity authority, has indelibly labeled *ageism*.

8 Somehow, even well-intentioned potential employers casually assume that age renders these folks—lawyers, teachers, writers, doctors, accountants, social workers—suddenly incapable of tasks more demanding than reading to third graders.

9 Marc Freedman, founder of Civic Ventures, a think tank and **incubator** of ideas about later years, has just published a book titled "**Encore**," describing examples of satisfying second and third careers, but that term applies to jobs, not people.

> **incubator** *n.* a place or situation that permits or encourages the formation and development, as of new ideas 温床，允许或鼓励新的想法产生并发展的地方或形式
>
> **encore** *n.* an additional performance in response to the demand of an audience 再来一次

10 In a *New York Times* report last month on graying suburbs, Sam Roberts offered a clever coinage: *suppies*, playing off the '80s acronym for young urban professionals. But even that applies only to some of the millions in this eighth age of life.

11 "We struggle with this in everything we write," says William H. Frey, a visiting scholar at the Brookings Institution. "We get a lot of pushback when we use 'pre-seniors' to describe people in their mid-50s. 'That's not me!' they say."

12 There is probably no single acceptable term—because no single term can embrace so vast and varied a population. The ultimate answer will most likely be a suite of functional and factual terms, like the typology scholars use to distinguish between the young old, 65 to 80; the old old, 80 to 90; the oldest old, 90 to 99; and centenarians. Terms like these, though somewhat awkward, are apt to enter common usage as society faces up to the new age of age.

Necessity is the mother of locution.

13   Modern life keeps adding zeroes. *Millionaire* once meant rich. Now it describes the owner of a two-bedroom apartment in Manhattan. For a time, *billionaire* was an exclusive label; *Forbes* magazine now counts almost a thousand of them around the world. Meanwhile, Bill Gates and others have a head start toward becoming *trillionaires*.

14   _____E_____. In the 1960s, Lyndon Johnson worried about being the first president to ask Congress for a $100 billion federal budget. Next year, President Bush's budget request may exceed $3 trillion.

15   How, in this 13-figure world, do you now characterize immense amounts? For the moment, *zillions* will probably suffice, and then, when that pales into insignificance, there's always *gazillions*.

> **zillion(s)** *n.* very large indeterminate number 极大数目
> **gazillion(s)** *n.* (infml) an indefinitely large number 极大数目

(Words: 734)

• Second Reading •

Directions: Read the text again more carefully to find enough information for Exercises I, II, III, IV & V.

Exercise I Understanding Text Organization

Directions: You may find there are a few sentences (segments) missing from the passage. Read the article through and decide where the following sentences should go.

1. Language has not yet caught up with life.
2. Still other terms fail because they are too narrow.
3. Not so long ago, *trillion* was a figurative exaggeration for fantastically costly.
4. *Oldsters* and *golden agers* are patronizing, targets for comics.
5. Some people have always lived to be very old, but never before have so many lived so much longer and stronger.

Exercise II Multiple-Choice Questions

Directions: Please choose the best answer from the four choices given.

1. Shakespeare would have the problem to call the millions of old people now because_____.

A. there are always people living to be very old

B. there are more than seven ages of man

C. there are less than seven ages of man

D. never before have so many people lived longer and stronger

2. We can infer the meaning of "wellderly" as _____.

   A. well-off
   B. wealthy and old
   C. robust and old
   D. kind and old

3. *Retirees* is an imperfect generalization for the elder because it encompasses which of the following group of people?

   A. Those who retire in their 40s.

   B. Those who continue to work after 70s.

   C. Both A and B.

   D. Neither A nor B.

4. They bridle even at inoffensive standbys like *elders* and *older adults*. Which understanding is correct?

   A. They like the neutral terms and accept them.

   B. "Elders" and "older adults" are the alternatives for old people and they are derogatory.

   C. They went mad at being called "elders" or "older adults."

   D. People tend to insult them by calling them "elders" or "older adults."

5. Dr. Robert Butler, the longevity authority may define *ageism* as _____.

   A. discrimination against old people
   B. respect for old people
   C. problems caused by old age
   D. study of aging problems

Exercise III Word Matching

Directions: Please choose the supplied words to explain the original forms of the boldfaced words in the following sentences.

A. get angry   B. be enough   C. naming   D. cause   E. theory of types

1. But that witty distinction doesn't solve the larger **nomenclature** problem.
2. The ultimate answer will most likely be a suite of functional and factual terms, like the **typology** scholars use to distinguish between the young old, 65 to 80; the old old, 80 to 90; the oldest old, 90 to 99; and centenarians.
3. For the moment, *zillions* will probably **suffice**, and then, when that pales into insignificance, there's always *gazillions*.

4. Not out of denial or vanity but because the experience of older people shows that any such generalization *ignites* unthinking discrimination—what Dr. Robert Butler, the longevity authority, has indelibly labeled *ageism*.

5. They *bridle* even at inoffensive standbys like *elders* and *older adults*.

Exercise IV   Short-Answer Questions
Directions: Please answer the following questions briefly in your own words.

1. Have you read Shakespeare's passage "The Seven Ages of Man"? Try to get it to appreciate.
2. How do you understand the book's title "Encore"?
3. The author mentions that modern life keeps adding zeroes. How do you understand it? What problems may it bring to the society?

Exercise V   Discussion
Directions: Please discuss the following questions in pairs or groups.

1. Why do you think people are so sensitive to the issue of aging and the way they are being addressed by others?
2. Can you work out a proper term that will be accepted by all?

Text C

Why We Must Listen to Our Angry Teenagers

By Catherine O'Brien

1   By the time Nick Luxmoore visited Nathan at his immaculate family home, the 12-year-old had twice been excluded from school. The first time, Nathan had hurled furniture around the classroom and lashed out at the teacher trying to restrain him. He was sent home for a week and returned promising that it would not happen again. Three weeks later, it did. He hit a boy in the mouth before storming out, kicking the door so hard that its panels split. The deputy

head found him half an hour later behind the sports hall, clearly upset but claiming not to care. He was sent home for two weeks and Luxmoore, a psychotherapist and school counsellor, was called in to help everyone decide what to do.

2   At that initial meeting, surrounded by his mother's plumped cushions and glossy indoor plants, Nathan said very little. But over the ensuing weeks, Luxmoore was able to tease from him some of the trigger points for his outbursts—his grandmother's death, starting secondary school, changing teachers, his brother being born, the lizard escaping. Many of his experiences involved feelings which he had found impossible to put into words. Instead he learnt to be hard—hiding his emotions under a cloak of anger.

3   How many boys are like Nathan? A lot, to judge by the record number of pupils being expelled for violent behaviour—60 a day in London alone. Every few weeks, there are reports of teachers being punched, throttled or knocked unconscious. These assaults are at the extreme end of the spectrum, but all parents of teenagers know something of the confusion, rage and resentment that can burst from a previously mild-mannered child.

4   Luxmoore specialises in unpredictable adolescents. A former English and drama teacher (and father of two grown-up daughters), he has worked for the past six years as a counsellor for troubled pupils in Oxfordshire. He declares that the parent or teacher must first of all recognise anger. This may be fairly obvious with the window-smashers and door-slammers—but, says Luxmoore: "One young person might fail to do any course work, another might steal. And I've never worked with a self-harmer who wasn't also extremely angry."

5   Read through the case studies in Luxmoore's latest book and a common strand emerges. Unsurprisingly, many teens are coping with complex family situations—divorced or warring parents, absent fathers, new step-siblings. "Family conflict has no boundaries, which is why anger is as much of a problem in privileged schools as it is in those for the so-called deprived," he says.

6   For others, like Nathan, home life may be ostensibly calm but anger erupts because of a need to be understood. Luxmoore, 50, can relate to this from personal experience. At 15, he was almost expelled from his South Coast boarding school after a fight that got out of hand.

He recalls his anger "at not being listened to, at the bullying and people being shut up and put in their places." He says: "One of the most important things we can do is simply to recognise young people. Say hello—and ideally remember their names. Make them feel that they count."

7   Often during his working week, a group of difficult pupils will be herded into Luxmoore's room for what he terms "miracle work." They are invariably there under duress. They need focusing, and they also need a mechanism to vent their feelings. One of his favourite starting points is asking each person to complete the sentence: "One thing that irritates me is... " In the second round, "irritates" is replaced by "annoys," then by "angers" and finally everyone is asked to say what they hate.

8   "A lot of adults—parents and professionals—don't like that word. It upsets them and makes them nervous," Luxmoore says. "But young people hate a lot. They hate school, their parents, life. They hate intensely at times and their feelings are far better acknowledged than suppressed."

9   Luxmoore is wary of the trend towards anger management in schools. Yet some techniques, he acknowledges, have a "grain of good thinking in them." Pastoral support plans follow recalcitrant pupils through the day with a report system that heightens awareness of their behaviour and achievements. Time-out cards, often coloured red like a football referee's—can be given to those prone to flare-ups. When pupils feel that their anger is bubbling to the surface, they show the red card, which then allows them to exit the class and cool off. "The good thing is that, in showing the card, the pupil is at least recognising what he or she is feeling. But there can be no quick fixes: to resolve the anger, you have to get to the root of it."

10   His own techniques vary from case to case, and often between boys and girls. "The struggle for boys is usually to dare to admit they have feelings in common. Such is their homophobic anxiety that they perceive any emotional connection as 'well gay'. So they insist that they are different, while yearning to belong."

11   "With girls, it is the reverse: the tyranny is about being the same and the real dare is to disagree. Girls are also taught to feel sad rather than angry. They cry tears of rage, and my job is to try to separate the two. Sometimes, we set up a crying chair and an angry chair and move between them so that the two feelings don't get muddled up."

12   Luxmoore did months of counselling with Nathan, and recalls: "Sometimes things are unfair, like the dice when it refuses to come up with a six. In games and in life we risk humiliation and defeat and we don't always get what we deserve. A big part of helping young people like Nathan to understand anger is making those feelings normal."

13   "Anger is healthy. Of course, the way it is expressed matters hugely. Smashing things and

swearing at people are not acceptable. But out of anger can come the determination to change things for the better."

14 The most helpful thing we can do for an angry young person, Luxmoore says, is to listen. "When I'm trying to understand young people I say things like: 'Tell me more so that I'll understand... I'm beginning to understand... Hang on, I don't completely understand.' I ask questions. I get things wrong and try again. Really understanding someone demands imagination and empathy—it may be harder than it seems. But keep going and you will see that, for the young person, the relief of being understood at long last can be an end in itself."

(Words: 1125)

Exercise I Discussion

Directions: Please discuss the following questions in pairs or groups.

1. Why do teenagers tend to quarrel with their parents?
2. "Anger is healthy. Of course, the way it is expressed matters hugely." How do you understand this sentence?
3. What is the perfect pattern of relationship between parents and adolescent children?

Exercise II Writing

Directions: All the articles in this unit are concerned with generation issues. Choose one that you are most interested in and write a composition on it in about 150 words.

UNIT FIVE

PARADOXES IN REALITY

Target of the Unit

☞ To get a glimpse of some paradoxes in reality and better understand the complexity of life
☞ To practice reading skills
☞ To enlarge your vocabulary

1) LEAD IN

Directions: In this unit, you will read 3 passages about various paradoxes we humans might encounter and experience in reality: having a yearning for the dirtiest place while feeling a sense of loss in the cleanest place, empathetic persons being indifferent, and friendship being toxic. All these paradoxes reflect the complexity of life and human nature. Try to understand them and relate the message conveyed in the articles to your own life.

2) DISCUSSION

In your life, what paradoxical matters have you personally experienced? What did you learn from them?

Text A

The Cleanest Place on Earth—and the Dirtiest

By Angela Palmer

Warming-up Exercises

☞ Which city or place do you think is the dirtiest or cleanest in China or in the world? Why do you think so?
☞ What kind of city or place do you think is the most habitable? Why?

• First reading •

Directions: Now please read the following passage as fast as you can and then get the exercises done as required.

1   In March, I dreamed that I went to the most polluted place in the world and then to the cleanest. In the dream, I wore identical white outfits, which were then exhibited side by side in a **stark** white gallery. When I awoke, I resolved to enact my dream. It seemed like madness: I was preparing for my final show at the Royal College of Art in London and was intending to show work based on CT scans of an ancient Egyptian mummy. But the sense of "mission" was overwhelming. I jettisoned my original plans: this was to be it.

> **stark** *adj.* complete or utter; extreme 完全的；极端的
> **flask** *n.* a small container, such as a bottle, having a narrow neck and usually a cap 水瓶
> **filter** *n.* a device containing porous materials, especially one used to extract impurities from air or water 过滤装置

2   Research into the world's most polluted place pointed to Linfen, a city 485 miles (780 km) south-west of Beijing, lying in a bowl in Shanxi province's coal-mining region. Linfen was named by the World Bank last year as having the worst air quality on earth. It features alongside Chernobyl in the Blacksmith Institute's list of the 10 most polluted places in the world and tops the list of most polluted cities compiled by China's own state environmental protection authority.

3   In contrast, Cape Grim, at the north-western tip of Tasmania, lays claim to both the cleanest air and water in the planet, largely due to the Roaring Forties, the winds that sweep in over the Southern Ocean. It is home to the Australian government's baseline air pollution station, whose unique "Air Library" collects samples as a "pure air" yardstick for scientists worldwide. I wanted to bring back this clean air—as well as the filthy air—and quickly these plans began to preoccupy me.

4   Fresh air must surely be the most precious commodity of the future. Unlike the world's land and water, air cannot be owned—there are no borders to confine it. Yet we knowingly infect it and in doing so infect our neighbours across continents. To try to gauge the difference between the two places, I left on my adventure with two pre-evacuated glass **flasks** donated by the Australian government to collect the air, a personal air pump to amass particulates on **filters**, and canisters to

bring back water samples. In addition, there were two white linen shirts, white jeans and white cotton shoes, from Zara and Marks & Spencer, outfits which would act as blank manuscripts on which the air of each place would inscribe itself.

5 I reached Linfen to find the sun shining—darkness hadn't descended at noon as was claimed in some reports. No one was even wearing a mask. Were they **oblivious** to the poisons they were **ingesting**? Despite the many citizens suffering from respiratory diseases, lead poisoning and disorders caused by high levels of **arsenic** in more than half of the city's well water, there was no discernible sign of crisis or discontent. When I asked about pollution, people simply shrugged their shoulders, as if the question were pointless.

6 In the streets, men were playing *Go* at makeshift tables, young and old shop staff were throwing themselves into a highly skilled game of **shuttlecock** football, children were skipping and men and women were busily **kneading** great wads of dough. The place throbbed with life. The streets, the walls and the oil drum "cookers" were caked in layers of filth and **grime**, and from time to time, great **wafts** of odour, like rotten eggs, would roll over everything. At night I left my hotel window propped open in order to run my air pump filter to collect the **particulates**. As I lay in bed, I thought of the chemicals, the unseen enemy, filling my room.

> **oblivious** *adj.* lacking conscious awareness; unmindful 不知不觉的，不自觉的
> **ingest** *v.* to take into the body by the mouth for digestion or absorption 咽下
> **arsenic** *n.* symbol As, a highly poisonous metallic element 符号 As, 砷: 一种有剧毒的金属元素
> **shuttlecock** *n.* a small rounded piece of cork or rubber with a conical crown of feathers or plastic, used in badminton, also called bird, birdie 羽毛球
> **knead** *v.* to mix and work into a uniform mass, as by folding, pressing, and stretching with the hands 揉成，捏制
> **grime** *n.* black dirt or soot, especially such dirt clinging to or ingrained in a surface 沉积在表面的灰尘或烟黑
> **waft** *n.* sth, such as an odor, that is carried through the air（气味、风等的）一阵，一股
> **particulates** *n.pl.* a minute separate particle, as of a granular substance or powder 微粒
> **pristine** *adj.* remaining free from dirt or decay; clean 新鲜的或清洁的，干净的

7 After four days in Linfen, I set off for Cape Grim in Tasmania. Here the rubble and diggers and filth were replaced with Constable-style landscapes. The trees were the height of Linfen's tower blocks. Great stretches of beach lay empty, with only the occasional footprint in the sand to suggest any trace of human life. An hour's driving was only finally interrupted by a sign advertising bottled water: "Cape Grim, Home of the Purest Air and Water on Earth, Jim's Plains."

8 After I had captured the air from Cape Grim in my flask, I tried to talk to the locals in Smithton, the nearest town, a 20-minute drive away. I had hoped to document the parallel lives of people living in such different atmospheric conditions, but while my **pristine** clothes and

air filters remained **unblemished**, so did the pages of my notebook. The Tasmanian reserve was daunting. Barely a soul was in the street. People were tucked away in their houses behind net curtains. Picket fences surrounded properties. Perfectly **manicured** gardens were adorned with plastic swans. I began to feel lonely, and, as the days passed, to yearn for the sense of community that had been so electrifying in the streets of Linfen.

> **unblemished** *adj.* not marred or impaired by any flaw 没有瑕疵的，未被破坏的
> **manicure** *v.* to clip or trim evenly and closely 修剪

(Words: 859)

• Second Reading •

Directions: Read the text again more carefully to find enough information for Exercises I, II & III.

Exercise I   True or False

Directions: Please state whether the following statements are true or not (T/F) according to the text.

1. Linfen was named by the World Environmental Protection Organization as having the worst air quality on earth.
2. Cape Grim lays claim to both the cleanest air and water in the world.
3. Clean water will become the most precious commodity in the future.
4. The author set out to gauge air quality with special glass flasks donated by the American government.
5. Since many people suffered from respiratory diseases in Linfen, some of the citizens were wearing masks.
6. When asked about pollution, people in Linfen did not think of it as a serious problem.
7. Although heavily polluted, people in Linfen lead a lively and busy life.
8. In Cape Grim, the trees were green, however quite short.
9. The author successfully recorded the parallel life in Cape Grim as she had done in Linfen.
10. In Cape Grim, perfectly manicured gardens were adorned with real swans.

Exercise II Word Inference

Directions: Often you can guess the meaning of a word/expression by reading the words around it. Please read the given sentence to see how each word/expression in bold type is used in the text. Then choose the answer that is closest in meaning to the bold-faced word/expression.

1. When I awoke, I resolved to **enact** my dream.
   A. realize   B. recall   C. forget   D. thought about

2. In the dream, I wore **identical** white outfits.
   A. usually   B. familiar   C. the same   D. plain

3. But the sense of "mission" was overwhelming, I **jettisoned** my original plan.
   A. improved   B. threw away   C. carried out   D. worked out

4. Cape Grim **lays claim to** both the cleanest air and water in the planet.
   A. declares to have   B. asks the right to have
   C. boasts of   D. possesses

5. The unique "Air Library" in Cape Grim collects samples as a "pure air" **yardstick** for scientists worldwide.
   A. measuring rope   B. example
   C. sample   D. standard measurement

6. Angela set out to **gauge** the air quality difference between the two places.
   A. discover   B. measure   C. contrast   D. work out

7. In addition, the white shirts, jeans and cotton shoes could act as blank manuscripts on which the air of each place would **inscribe** itself.
   A. mark   B. impress   C. stamp   D. prescribe

8. Despite the many citizens suffering from respiratory diseases, lead poisoning and disorders caused by high levels of arsenic, there was no **discernible** sign of crisis or discontent.
   A. caution   B. foreseeable   C. perceptible   D. warning

9. In the streets, children were skipping and men and women were busily kneading great wads of dough. The place **throbbed** with life.
   A. was living   B. was jumping   C. was beaten   D. was dynamic

10. I began to feel lonely, and, as the days passed, to yearn for the sense of community that had been so **electrifying** in the streets of Linfen.
    A. suffocating   B. thrilling   C. threatening   D. impressing

Exercise III　Discussion

Directions: Please discuss the following questions in pairs or groups.

1. Do you agree with the author's opinion that "Fresh air must surely be the most precious commodity in the future"? Why or why not?
2. Do you think pollution is such an urgent issue that threatens the survival of human beings as a whole? What can people do to solve this problem?

Text B

Somewhere Deep Down, We Still Care. Don't We?

By Tony Long

Warming-up Exercises

☞ What's your attitude toward misery and cruelty in life?
☞ What will you do if you find people in danger?

• First reading •

Directions: Now please read the following passage as fast as you can and summarize the main idea.

1　　Flower, the **matriarch** of a **meerkat** clan living in the Kalahari Desert, died a few weeks ago, killed by a cobra as she defended her young from the **marauding** snake.

2　　This is not news to the viewers of Animal Planet's Meerkat Manor, who knew Flower from the popular British nature series and endured watching as the **plucky** mammal

> **matriarch** *n.* a woman who rules a family, clan, or tribe 女族长,女家长
> **meerkat** *n.* a small southern African mongoose, especially the suricate（南非）海岛猫鼬
> **maraud** *v.* to rove and raid in search of booty 劫掠，四处流窜抢劫
> **plucky** *adj.* having or showing courage and spirit in trying circumstances 有勇气的，有胆量的

61

bloated up and died after being bitten in the attack, which was filmed by the Animal Planet crew.

The Whiskers' Clan

Flower Whiskers

3   The *New York Times* used Flower's death, and the public outpouring of grief that it provoked, as an opportunity to **opine** on the dysfunctional state of modern emotional life. (According to the *Times*, internet message boards lit up with people **mired** in the various stages of grief and assorted irrational behavior, with many demanding to know why the film crew failed to intervene on Flower's behalf.)

4   I've never seen the show, didn't know Flower existed, and have nothing to offer on the specifics of the fatal encounter.   A .

5   What it got me to thinking about, other than I'm glad I'm not a meerkat facing down a cobra, was how my own attitude toward violence and suffering has changed over the years.

6   I've been in the news business for a long time. I remember as a young editor being deeply affected by certain stories I'd seen, often involving abject human misery and cruelty, only to hear the older guys on the desk cracking tasteless jokes and laughing about those same stories. I put this down to the "cop mentality" that a lot of reporters and editors develop. Constant exposure to the **seamy** underbelly of human existence, which pervades certain aspects of our business, forces you grow a thick skin. Some of it is **bravado**, for sure, but not all of it.

> **bloat** *v.* to become swollen or inflated 使肿胀，变肿或膨胀
> **opine** *v.* to hold or state as an opinion 持有意见或发表意见
> **mire** *v.* to hinder, entrap, or entangle as if in mire 使受困扰，使阻碍、牵绊或纠缠（如陷入泥沼一般）
> **seamy** *adj.* sordid; base 丑恶的，肮脏的，卑鄙的
> **bravado** *n.* （usu unnecessary or false）display of boldness 逞能；虚张声势

7   B . "Family of six slaughtered in Alabama trailer park." "Ferryboat carrying religious pilgrims capsizes in Java Sea—hundreds die." Yeah? Wow. When's lunch?

8   When the suffering is right in front of me, it's different. When I can attach a face to

something bad that's happening, I'm as empathetic as they come. If I can help, I will. Had I been the cameraman at Flower's last battle, I probably would have attempted something stupidly heroic. (Although maybe not; snakes give me the creeps.)

9   But I never saw Flower, so her death is an abstraction to me. __C__.

10   So I read the *Times* story with interest, because it struck me that many of the same people who went into mourning over Flower's death, a death which after all merely affirms the fact that nature is cruelly indifferent to suffering, would be unlikely to shed the same tears for an anonymous murder victim who turns up on the evening news. I'm not talking about a bunch of jaded reporters here. I'm talking about all of us. Or a lot of us, anyway.

11   The makers of Meerkat Manor humanized Flower (they gave her a name, didn't they?) and gave their viewers an emotional investment in this particular animal. __D__. The poor **sod** who gets himself shot up in an alley and winds up on News at 6 doesn't matter nearly as much, because you'd never heard of him before you poured your last beer.

12   I suppose that's only natural. The thing that bothers me, though, is an associated condition: I think people are becoming desensitized to violence and suffering at a much earlier age these days. And I'm pretty sure it has a lot do with the way we've accepted violence, and even glorified it, in popular culture. In simple terms, Quentin Tarantino has a lot to answer for.

> **sod** *n.* a fellow; a guy 家伙
> **proliferation** *n.* rapid increase in the number or amount of sth 迅速的增长；扩散
> **at large** *prep.phr.* as a whole; in general 全体，普遍地
> **paean** *n.* a fervent expression of joy or praise 赞歌，欢乐歌
> **gratuitous** *adj.* given or received without cost or obligation; free 无偿的,免费或无需承担义务和费用地得到或接受的
> **wisecracking** *v.p.p.* making smart or clever remarks（often unkind）说俏皮话，说风凉话
> **goombah** *n.* a companion or an associate, especially an older friend who acts as a patron, a protector, or an adviser 同伴或同事，特指以赞助人、保护人或顾问身份出现的年长的朋友
> **squealer** *n.* animal that squeals 尖声嚎叫的动物

13   There are studies out there purporting to prove the correlation between the **proliferation** of violent content in films and videogames and a corresponding rise in aggressive behavior and violence in society **at large**. I'm not especially interested in the statistical proof one way or the other. I've seen and heard enough anecdotal evidence to know that it's true.

14   Whether it's a crude slasher movie, or a kid wasting virtual victims in front of a glowing screen in a darkroom or one of Tarantino's artlessly stylish **paeans** to **gratuitous** violence, there is a cause-and-effect at play here. If watching some smartass, **wisecracking goombah** torture a lowlife **squealer** to death with a blowtorch is just another day at the office, well then, Hollywood, we got us a little problem.

15   __E__. (In other words, it doesn't involve censorship.) But it probably does involve a complete change in our collective attitude. If you keep lapping up garbage, they'll keep

dishing it out. If you demand **filet mignon**, you'll get that. The tricky part, of course, is that one person's filet is another person's garbage.

> **filet mignon** *n.* （US） small tender piece of beef without bones, cut from a sirloin （牛的）里脊
> **perdition** *n.* loss of the soul; eternal damnation 毁灭，灵魂的失落，永久的罚入地狱
> **quarter** *v.* to dismember （a human body） into four parts 将（人体）肢解成四分

16 How will we know when the road to **perdition** has turned onto the road to recovery? Maybe when Tarantino adapts Jane Austen's *Pride and Prejudice* and resists the temptation to show Mr. Darcy being drawn and **quartered**. Maybe then.

(Words: 907)

• Second Reading •

Directions: Read the text again more carefully to find enough information for Exercises I, II, III, IV & V.

Exercise I Understanding Text Organization

Directions: You may find there are a few sentences (segments) missing from the passage. Read the article through and decide where the following sentences should go.

1. Consequently, I feel nothing. Or, at least, very little.
2. So her death, coming as violently as it did (and nobly—she was protecting her young, remember), is bound to evoke an emotional response.
3. But Flower's grim fate and the reaction it provoked did have an effect on me.
4. I don't know what the solution to the problem is.
5. Eventually, without really being aware of it, the same thing happened to me. Stories that used to upset me barely registered a reaction.

Exercise II Multiple-Choice Questions

Directions: Please choose the best answer from the four choices given.

1. Flower, the matriarch of a meerkat clan, was killed by _____.
   A. another meerkat   B. the Animal Planet crew
   C. a poisonous snake   D. a hunter

2. Who seemed to have been grieved by the tragic death of Flower?
   A. The Animal Planet crew.   B. Editors of the *New York Times*.
   C. The author of this article.   D. Many viewers of Meerkat Manor.
3. "Constant exposure to the seamy underbelly of human existence, which pervades certain aspects of our business, forces *you grow a thick skin*." What does the italicized part mean?
   A. Become not easily upset by criticism.   B. Become not easily influenced by others.
   C. Become hardened.   D. Become shameless.
4. According to the author, the reason why Flower's death to many people matter more than that of a murder victim is that _____.
   A. they knew much about her but nothing about him
   B. she was a rare animal needing special protection
   C. he was a gangster who deserved the fate
   D. he was not as heroic as she was
5. Which of the following is NOT mentioned as a factor which makes people desensitized to violence and suffering at a much earlier age?
   A. Popular culture.
   B. Jane Austen's *Pride and Prejudice*.
   C. Quentin Tarantino's films.
   D. Videogames.

Exercise III   Word Matching

Directions: Please choose the supplied words to explain the original forms of the boldfaced words in the following sentences.

A. sympathetic   B. unknown by name   C. overturn   D. claim   E. wretched

1. I remember as a young editor being deeply affected by certain stories I'd see, often involving **abject** human misery and cruelty, …
2. "Ferryboat carrying religious pilgrims **capsizes** in Java Sea—hundreds die."
3. When I can attach a face to something bad that's happening, I'm as **empathetic** as they come.
4. … would be unlikely to shed the same tears for an **anonymous** murder victim who turns up on the evening news.
5. There are studies out there **purporting** to prove the correlation between the proliferation of violent content in films and videogames…

Exercise IV   Short-Answer Questions

Directions: Please answer the following questions briefly in your own words.

1. What is the "cop mentality"?
2. Why did many people react emotionally to Flower's death?
3. Who does the author think should be responsible for the rise of aggressive behavior and violence in society at large?

Exercise V   Discussion

Directions: Please discuss the following questions in pairs or groups.

1. What's people's general reaction to miserable stories of strangers? Do they react the same way to the miseries of people they know well? Why?
2. What roles do you think the media play in the proliferation of violence? And what should they do to solve the problem?

Text C

Could Friendships Be Ruining Your Life?

By Tim Shipman

1 Rhona Rogers had been friends with Sally Thompson for more than 20 years. They grew up together in a small town in California. They played together, went to school together, swore they would be friends forever. Then one day, earlier this year, Rhona realised that she couldn't stand Sally.

2 Sally constantly put her down; she was rude about Rhona's mother and her other friends. For two decades, Rhona had made excuses for Sally, but now just being around her made Rhona feel anxious.

3 Realising that one of the most important relationships in her life had gone bad, Rhona—a 32-year-old estate agent—did what any self-respecting American with issues would do: she went to relationship therapy. But this was a different kind of therapy.

4   For years, the American self-help industry has told romantic couples how to repair their rifts. But now, counsellors are being called in by troubled patients who want to know how to ditch those "friends" who are ruining their lives.

5   More than 10,000 registered psychologists and counsellors are offering sessions on relationships with friends in America. Someone needing their advice can expect to pay anywhere between $75 and $200 for an hour-long session.

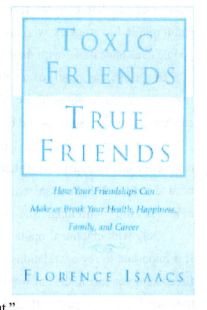

6   "Sally was always making snide comments," says Rhona. "For years, I felt she couldn't mean what she said—and then I realised she did. I saw someone and she helped me realise that Sally was a toxic friend. I cut her out."

7   The phrase "toxic friends" is becoming commonplace and has been recognised by the American Psychological Association.

8   The phenomenon has even received the ultimate popular endorsement—becoming the subject of a recent edition of Oprah Winfrey's talk show.

9   The self-help industry has also not been slow to get in on the act. A succession of books with such titles as "Toxic Friends/True Friends" and "A Smart Girl's Guide to Friendship," have hit the American bestseller lists.

10   Among those writers whose books compete for space on the self-help shelves is Mike Albo, a performance artist from New York. He had been troubled by a friend whose back-handed compliments were destroying his confidence. So he set about writing his manual, *The Underminer*, with his flatmate.

11   "In this culture, people are competitive but polite at the same time, so they undermine you with a smile on their face," Mr Albo said. "In other ages, people would have hit each other with clubs; we just have someone saying to us: 'Oh, you look tired. Are you OK?'"

12   "People say: 'Oh, I just saw your ex-girlfriend, she looks beautiful,' or 'Oh, you're drinking. I realised it was making me feel bad but it's so great that you can still do that.' Underminers latch onto your weaknesses. My favourite is: 'Do you still like your new haircut?'"

13   "In a romantic relationship, when it reaches that stage, you have an argument and split up."

14   The realisation that friends can be the cause of unhappiness is fuelling a rapid rise in the

number of people consulting therapists. Dr Judith Orloff, a psychiatrist at the University of California in Los Angeles, who also runs a private practice, says: "Probably 90 per cent of the people I see have issues with their friends."

15   Dr Orloff, the author of a self-help book, *Positive Energy*, said: "Energy drain comes from all our relationships. There is now a much greater appreciation of the effect that friends can have, as well as spouses and bosses."

16   It is a point on which her British colleagues agree. Christine Northam, a relationship counsellor and therapist for Relate, says that to maintain our emotional health, friendships need to be frequently re-assessed. "Analysing friendships is increasingly important in all types of relationship counselling," she says.

17   "Only with emotional maturity can we see ourselves and our relationships more clearly. It is important to review relationships and sometimes that leads us to see that the reason your friend kept you late in the bar was not because they were enjoying your company, but because they wanted you to deal with their issues. It is easy to become sucked into those kinds of friendships, but they tend to leave us feeling exhausted and depressed. In good friendship, there must be a level of reciprocity."

18   "It can seem a bit ruthless to cut loose these friendships, but sometimes, all we need to do is put boundaries around 'toxic' friends: keep them in our lives but see them less frequently."

19   The consequences of not dealing with "toxic" friends can be dangerous. A recent study, published in the *Annals of Behavioural Medicine*, found that when participants merely saw a person who was an "ambivalent friend"—one who upsets you as often as they please you—their heart rates and blood pressure increased.

20   According to counsellors, these toxic friends come in several forms. In addition to the passive aggressive underminer, who delivers barbs dressed up as friendly inquiries, there is the naysayer, who undermines you more obviously, the plan-breaker, who ditches you at the last minute, and peer pressurers who won't let you go home when you want to.

21   They all agree it's tougher for women. Jan Yager, the author of *When Friendship Hurts: How to Deal with Friends Who Betray, Abandon, or Wound You*, says: "Males, having a much lower threshold for complications in friendships, will disengage themselves from a negative friendship more easily, and faster, than women."

22   Dr Orloff said that women friends can become "energy vampires" like the "sob sister who keeps you on the phone for two hours with problems but no solutions and who leaves you exhausted."

23   Jennifer, a 33-year-old nursery school teacher, turned to her friend Patricia when she found her marriage collapsing after the birth of her son. Patricia also had a bad-tempered

husband and the two women discussed whether to leave home. "We would talk on the phone every day, moaning about how horrible our husbands were and what we had done to deserve this," said Jennifer.

24   Jennifer divorced and went into therapy, Patricia did not. Now they barely speak. Jennifer's therapist convinced her she was attracted to abusive relationships—both romantic and friendly—and should put an end to both.

25   "It's like we only bonded through the pain," she says. "It doesn't seem like she wants to hear my good news now that things are better. Our relationship was at its best when we were at our worst."

26   Dr Orloff advises those with toxic friends to "recognise it—don't blame yourself or think you're neurotic—honour your own intuition. With friends, you can tell someone what's bothering you. If they don't listen, it's OK to stop returning their calls."

27   Not everyone is convinced that therapy is the answer. Mike Albo says that the self-help industry has provided underminers with a subtle language for convincing friends that they have a psychological problem.

28   "One thing that worries me about friendship counselling is that underminers prevail in the self-help society," he said. "Without therapy, people wouldn't say: 'I'm worried about you. Are you making the right choices?'"

29   Debbie Mandel has another warning for those confronting toxic friends: "Listen to their side of it because perhaps it's you who is toxic."

(Words: 1188)

Additional Reading

Friend Prototypes

Passive aggressive underminer   The friend who uses their knowledge of you to subtly undermine you, often making barbed comments about your appearance or habits cloaked in a veil of concern

Example: Edie Britt from "Desperate Housewives"

The constant talker   The friend who hogs every conversation and wants to be the centre of attention, with you in their orbit and shadow

Example: David Brent from "The Office"

The drama queen   The friend who elevates every minor setback into a major crisis, who is convinced that she's going to be fired because the boss didn't smile at her

Example: Ally McBeal from "Ally McBeal"

The naysayer The friend who dismisses your hopes and dreams as unrealistic and is generally negative about your plans; The classic "glass half-empty" individual

Example: Blanche Hunt in "Coronation Street"

The peer pressurer The friend who imposes their need for fun and attention over your best interest, who knows that you have a job interview tomorrow morning but pressures you to drink until midnight

Example: DCI Gene Hunt from "Life on Mars"

The plan breaker The unreliable friend who agrees to go out for dinner but then ditches you at the last minute because they got a better offer

Example: Frasier Crane from "Frasier"

The sob sister The friend who saps your energy by whining all the time, who would rather complain about the things in his or her life than fix them, dragging you into a culture of victimhood and using you as a therapist

Example: Ian Beale, from "EastEnders"

Exercise I Discussion

Directions: Please discuss the following questions in pairs or groups.

1. Do you have the same friendship problem mentioned in the passage? Did you ever turn to self-help industry to work your problem out? How did you solve your problem in the end?
2. Will you avoid toxic friends? If yes, how will you do it without hurting them?
3. Do you think genial friendship ever exists between men and women?

Exercise II Writing

Directions: Have you encountered dilemmas in your life? How did you manage to pull through them? Write a composition to tell about your experience of tackling a dilemma in about 150 words.

PEOPLE'S PLACE IN SOCIETY

Target of the Unit

☞ To get a better understanding of the relationship between people and the society they live in
☞ To practice reading skills
☞ To enlarge your vocabulary

1) LEAD IN

Directions: In this unit, you will read 3 passages about the place and well-being of people in the contemporary society. Though focusing on different issues, they all convey a people-first message and indicate from different angles what governments and citizens can do to make this world a better place to live in. Please see whether the notions and practices are applicable to China.

2) DISCUSSION

What elements make up a desirable society? And what roles should governments and citizens respectively play to raise the overall quality of life in a society?

Text A

Setting Happiness as a National Goal

By Richard Layard

Warming-up Exercises

☞ Are you happy with your present life? What makes you happy or unhappy in life?
☞ What or who do you think is most important in your life?

First reading

Directions: Now please read the following passage as fast as you can and summarize the main idea.

1 The best society is the one where the people are the happiest, and the best policy is the one that produces the greatest happiness. So argued great eighteenth century thinkers like Jeremy Bentham, and their admirable views did much to inspire the social reforms of the century that followed. But in many cases it was difficult to apply the principle, because so little was known about what makes people happy. However, the last 30 years have seen a major scientific revolution, and we now know much more about what causes happiness—using the results of psychology and neuroscience.

2 The first thing we know is that in the last 50 years average happiness has not increased at all in Britain, nor in the United States, despite massive increases in living standards. This is because above an average income of about $19,500 per head, richer societies are no happier than poorer societies. Richer people are, of course, on average happier than poorer people in the same society, but this is largely because people compare their incomes with other people. If everyone gets richer, they feel no better off.

> **neuroscience** *n.* the study of the brain and nervous system, including molecular neuroscience, cellular neuroscience, cognitive neuroscience, psychophysics, computational modeling and diseases of the nervous system 神经学
>
> **Scandinavian** *adj.* of or relating to Scandinavia or to its peoples, languages, or cultures 斯堪的纳维亚的，其民族、语言和文化的或与之有关的

3 In rich societies, what really affects happiness is the quality of personal relationships. Always at the top comes the quality of family life or other close personal relationships. Then comes work—having it (if you want it) and enjoying the meaning and comradeship it can bring. And then comes relationships with friends and strangers in the street.

4 Some societies are much happier than others, and Scandinavian countries always come out near the top. This is largely because people trust each other more there than in other places. In Britain and the United States, the number of people who believe that "most other people can be trusted" has halved in the last 50 years, and this reflects the growth of an individualism that makes personal success more important than almost anything else.

5 These facts call for a revolution in how we think about ourselves and about how the government can help us to flourish. It becomes clear that faster economic growth is not the most important objective for a society. We should not sacrifice human relationships nor

peace of mind for the sake of higher living standards, which will be growing anyway.

6   This insight should affect all areas of public policy. I cannot argue each proposal here, though they are argued in my book on *Happiness: Lessons from a New Science*. Let me just set down a few proposals rather boldly.

7   The most important thing we can affect is the values that our children acquire. Schools should teach children systematically that the secret of a happy life is in giving to other people. Evidence-based programs exist for doing this and should become a part of the core curriculum.

8   The least happy people in our society are people with a record of mental illness. Three-quarters of people with depression or hyper-anxiety receive no treatment, although psychological therapies exist that can cure over half of these terrible cases. Such therapies should be available for free.

9   Advertising makes people feel they need more and thus makes them less happy with what they have. One policy model is in Sweden, which bans advertising aimed at children under 12.

10 We should stop apologizing about taxes: They discourage us from working even harder and sacrificing further our relationships with family and friends. We should also persist with income redistribution, since an extra pound or dollar gives more happiness to poor people than to the rich. That argument also implies redistribution to the Third World.

11 We are in a new situation for mankind, where further wealth creation is now unnecessary for survival. If we want to become still happier, we need a new strategy from the one pursued over the last 50 years—we need to put human relationships first.

(Words: 677)

· Second Reading ·

Directions: Read the text again more carefully to find enough information for Exercises I, II & III.

Exercise I   True or False

Directions: Please state whether the following statements are true or not (T/F) according to the text.

1. The author believes that the best society is the one where people are richest in the world.
2. It's difficult to make people happy, because little is known about what makes people happy.
3. On account of massive increases in living standards, average happiness has increased in Britain and the US in the last 50 years.
4. Generally speaking, rich societies are happier than poor societies.
5. In rich societies, what affects happiness is the quality of personal relationships.
6. People in Scandinavian countries are generally happier than those in other countries.
7. In the author's opinion, schools should teach children that the secret of a happy life is to give rather than take.
8. The least happy people in the society are those with little money.
9. Advertising always provides people what they need.
10. People should persist with income redistribution in society.

Exercise II   Word Inference

Directions: Often you can guess the meaning of a word/expression by reading the words around it. Please read the given sentence to see how each word/expression in bold type is used in the text. Then choose the answer that is closest in meaning to the bold-faced word/expression.

1. Average happiness did not increase in Britain or the US, despite **massive** increases in living standards.
   A. lumpy   B. great   C. solid   D. fast
2. In rich societies, what really **affects** happiness is the quality of personal relationships.
   A. influences   B. effects   C. infects   D. affirm
3. These facts call for a revolution in how we think about ourselves and about how the government can help us to **flourish**.
   A. sprout   B. grow   C. flower   D. prosper
4. We should not **sacrifice** human relationships nor peace of mind for the sake of higher living standards.
   A. give off   B. give away   C. give up   D. give out
5. Let me just **set down** a few proposals.
   A. conclude   B. establish   C. apply   D. form

6. Evidence-based programs exist for doing this and should become a part of the core curriculum.

　　A. focuses　　　　B. objects　　　　C. principles　　　　D. courses

7. Three-quarters of people with depression or hyper-anxiety receive no treatment.

　　A. the state of being over-anxious　　B. overexcitement
　　C. the state of being overjoyed　　　 D. hypersensitivity

8. Psychological therapies can cure over half of these terrible cases.

　　A. methods　　　B. diagnosis　　　C. treatments　　　D. drugs

9. We should persist with income redistribution.

　　A. get rid of　　　　　　　　B. keep on with
　　C. argue with　　　　　　　　D. change

10. If we want to become still happier, we need a new strategy from the one pursued over the last 50 years.

　　A. went after　　B. followed　　C. carried out　　D. chased

Exercise III　Discussion

Directions: Please discuss the following questions in pairs or groups.

1. Do you regard happiness as an absolute individual affair or the interaction between people and society? Why?
2. In what way can a government help its people lead a happier life?

Text B

When Armed Citizens Patrol the Streets

By Tom A. Peter

Warming-up Exercises

☞ Do you feel safe walking in the streets alone 10 p.m. at night in your city?
☞ How do you comment on the civil security conditions in Beijing or other parts of China?

First reading

Directions: Now please read the following passage as fast as you can and summarize the main idea.

1   The Edgewood neighborhood near downtown New Haven, Conn., is probably one of the last places you'd expect to find residents patrolling the streets with pistols.

2   Turn-of-the-century carriage houses sport manicured lawns. Tall elm trees really do line Elm Street. And every night since youths beat up a **rabbi**'s son three weeks ago, members of the newly formed Edgewood Park Defense Patrol (EPDP) have been walking the streets at night. Roughly half of them have permits to carry concealed weapons and take a handgun on **patrol**.

3   Although there's nothing illegal about the practice, this **ratcheting** up of a traditional neighborhood watch worries local officials and national experts. Citizens rarely, if ever, have the training that police routinely receive to defuse volatile situations. But as budget woes and other priorities cause some localities to cut back neighborhood police patrols, advocates say that stepped-up citizen policing is an understandable response—although it's a risky one with guns.

> **rabbi** *n.* (abbr.) a person trained in Jewish law, ritual, and tradition and ordained for leadership of a Jewish congregation, especially one serving as chief religious official of a synagogue 拉比; a scholar qualified to interpret Jewish law 犹太学者
>
> **patrol** *n.* the act of moving about an area especially by an authorized and trained person or group, for purposes of observation, inspection, or security 巡逻
>
> **ratchet** *v.* to increase or decrease by increments 渐进,通常与 up, upward, down 或 downward 一起使用

4   ____A____. The situation started to improve in the late 1990s, in part due to neighborhood revitalization projects and New Haven police working closely with the community, says Avi Hack, a high school teacher and EPDP spokesman. But about five years ago, officers who used to work with Edgewood were reassigned—something Mr. Hack blames on the police chief—and "gangs of marauding youth" began harassing the neighborhood, he says.

5   After working with a variety of city officials and seeing no results, Hack says, "At a certain point we felt the only way to put the pressure on the mayor to either dismiss the police chief or get the police chief to do his job, which he seems incapable or unwilling to do, and ensure our own security was to form EPDP."

6   In an act of apparently random violence earlier this month, a group of youths attacked a local rabbi's adult son in his own home. Shortly afterward, members of the Jewish community along with some local African-Americans and others formed the EPDP.

7   __B__.

8   "I'm with you 100 percent!" shouts Tina Salters as the two pass by. Down the street, they're met with a scowl from Nancy Brown. "The police are working real hard and they don't need no one else coming out here with guns." Hack and Lynes don't carry guns.

9   Despite the EPDP criticism **heaped** on him, Chief Francisco Ortiz, a **staunch** advocate of community policing, says he "wholeheartedly" supports EPDP, though he made a point of officially not supporting their decision to carry weapons on patrol. He says neighborhood police patrols were reduced largely due to funding cuts.

10   __C__. But we lost those grants over the last six years," says Chief Ortiz. He explains the war on terror came at a price to community policing efforts that allowed officers enough time to work small beats and get to know the residents and their concerns. "The country shifted its focus. Like **Cyclops** with one eye, it took its eye off" community policing, he says.

11   Traditionally, community policing efforts encourage citizens to be the "eyes and ears" for police but to remain on the sidelines.

12   Neighborhood watch groups "should not be armed. Period. ... They are not trained; they are not educated in the laws, and it is distinctively a law-enforcement function," says Robbie Woodson, program manager of USAonWatch, an umbrella group that oversees the national Neighborhood Watch Program. "Leave the law-enforcement activities to law-enforcement officials—and part of that is armed patrols."

> **heap** v. to bestow in abundance or lavishly 将大量的（表扬或批评）加之于……
> **staunch** adj. firm and steadfast 坚定的
> **Cyclops** n. any of the three one-eyed Titans who forged thunderbolts for Zeus 泰坦神（为宙斯制造雷电的三个独眼泰坦神之一）
> **ingredient** n. an element in a mixture or compound; a constituent 成份
> **tote** v. (infml) to carry sth, especially regularly 携带，装备于某人身上
> **emeritus** adj. retired but retaining an honorary title corresponding to that held immediately before retirement 荣誉退休的，退休但仍荣誉保持退休前所拥有的职位

13   __D__. "The **ingredients** are here for a major problem," says Mr. Sliwa. "Lawyers are perched. The moment there's an incident with this patrol... you know there's going to be some civil suit filed claiming that their client's civil rights were violated by arms-**toting** posses."

14   Armed civilian patrols may have a hard time meeting the higher standards authorities have adopted over the past 40 years for how and when to use firearms, says Samuel Walker, **emeritus**

professor of criminal justice at the University of Nebraska at Omaha. "I'm not sure that these kinds of neighborhood patrols are aware of these kinds of rules.... The risk of them shooting someone who should not be shot is very high."

15   ____E____. In 2003, the "Oregon Rangers Association" raised eyebrows when it began patrolling Oregon's national forests armed with pistols and shotguns, intent on stopping crime in the wilderness and helping rangers stretched thin across the parks. With reports following 9/11 that terrorists planned to target Jewish neighborhoods, Rabbi Yakove Lloyd made international headlines when he announced his intent to organize civilian patrols armed with licensed firearms, baseball bats, and **walkie-talkies** through Jewish areas in Brooklyn, N.Y. The effort **fizzled** after a public outcry.

> **walkie-talkie** *n.* (pl) walkie-talkies; a battery-powered portable sending and receiving radio set 步话机
> **fizzle** *v.* (infml) to fail or end weakly, especially after a hopeful beginning 失败，夭折，尤指开始时很有希望但最终失败或结局不好

16   Crime overall in New Haven has fallen by 56 percent since 1990, according to New Haven's Uniform Crime Report.

(Words: 905)

• Second Reading •

Directions: Read the text again more carefully to find enough information for Exercises I, II, III, IV & V.

Exercise I Understanding Text Organization

Directions: You may find there are a few sentences (segments) missing from the passage. Read the article through and decide where the following sentences should go.

1. "We used to get a lot of grants to help [with community policing]—a couple million dollars a year.

2. Longtime residents say Edgewood was a peaceful place until the 1980s, when residents started moving out to the suburbs and drugs and prostitution moved in.

3. Although Curtis Sliwa, founder and president of the international community policing organization Guardian Angels, strongly supports EPDP, he, too, is concerned about members carrying weapons.

4. While armed civilian groups like the EPDP are rare, they are not unprecedented.

5. On this particular night, Hack and Gary Lynes—a retired musician—are on an hour-long patrol in matching black EPDP T-shirts.

Exercise II Multiple–Choice Questions

Directions: Please choose the best answer from the four choices given.

1. The EPDP was formed in _____.
   A. Connecticut   B. New York   C. Oregon   D. Nebraska
2. Who formed the EPDP?
   A. Local Jews.   B. Local police.
   C. Some local African-Americans. D. Both A and C.
3. According to the police chief, neighborhood police patrols were reduced simply because of _____.
   A. lower crime rates
   B. a lack of policemen
   C. funding cuts
   D. police's unpopularity with the community
4. Why are some people worried by the armed patrols of the EPDP?
   A. The members of the EPDP are not trained.
   B. The members of the EPDP are not educated in the laws.
   C. The members of the EPDP may shoot someone mistakenly.
   D. All of the above.
5. Which of the following didn't try to do armed civilian patrols?
   A. The EPDP.   B. USAonWatch.
   C. Oregon Rangers Association.   D. Rabbi Yakove Lloyd.

Exercise III Word Matching

Directions: Please choose the supplied words to explain the original forms of the boldfaced words in the following sentences.

A. area allocated to a policeman   B. trouble and annoy continually
C. unstable   D. problem   E. mow

1. Turn-of-the-century carriage houses sport **manicured** lawns.
2. Citizens rarely, if ever, have the training that police routinely receive to defuse **volatile** situations.

3. But as budget **woes** and other priorities cause some localities to cut back neighborhood police patrols, advocates say that stepped-up citizen policing is an understandable response—although it's a risky one with guns.

4. But about five years ago, officers who used to work with Edgewood were reassigned—something Mr. Hack blames on the police chief—and "gangs of marauding youth" began **harassing** the neighborhood, he says.

5. He explains the war on terror came at a price to community policing efforts that allowed officers enough time to work small **beats** and get to know the residents and their concerns.

Exercise IV   Short-Answer Questions

Directions: Please answer the following questions briefly in your own words.

1. What does EPDP stand for?
2. What triggered EPDP directly?
3. What could the sentence "Lawyers are perched." (Para. 13) mean?

Exercise V   Discussion

Directions: Please discuss the following questions in pairs or groups.

1. Name the safest and most dangerous city/place in China or in the world respectively. And then give your reasons.
2. Who are to blame for the increased violence and crimes in modern society?

Text C

Designing Cities for People, Rather than Cars...

By Lester R. Brown

1   As I was being driven through Tel Aviv from my hotel to a conference center a few years ago, I could not help but note the overwhelming presence of cars and parking lots. Tel Aviv, expanding from a small settlement a half-century ago to a city of some 3 million today,

evolved during the automobile era. It occurred to me that the ratio of parks to parking lots may be the best single indicator of the livability of a city—whether a city is designed for people or for cars.

2   The world's cities are in trouble. In Mexico City, Tehran, Bangkok, Shanghai, and hundreds of other cities, the quality of daily life is deteriorating. Breathing the air in some cities is equivalent to smoking two packs of cigarettes per day. In the United States, the number of hours commuters spend sitting in traffic going nowhere climbs higher each year.

3   In response to these conditions, we are seeing the emergence of a new urbanism. One of the most remarkable modern urban transformations has occurred in Bogotá, Colombia, where Enrique Peñalosa served as Mayor for three years, beginning in 1998. When he took office he did not ask how life could be improved for the 30 percent who owned cars; he wanted to know what could be done for the 70 percent—the majority—who did not own cars.

Peñalosa realized that a city that is a pleasant environment for children and the elderly would work for everyone. In just a few years, he transformed the quality of urban life with his vision of a city designed for people. Under his leadership, the city banned the parking of cars on sidewalks, created or renovated 1,200 parks, introduced a highly successful bus-based rapid transit system, built hundreds of kilometers of bicycle paths and pedestrian streets, reduced rush hour traffic by 40 percent, planted 100,000 trees, and involved local citizens directly in the improvement of their neighborhoods. In doing this, he created a sense of civic pride among the city's 8 million residents, making the streets of Bogotá in strife-torn Colombia safer than those in Washington, D.C.

4   Enrique Peñalosa observes that "high quality public pedestrian space in general and parks in particular are evidence of a true democracy at work." He further observes: "Parks and public space are also important to a democratic society because they are the only places where people meet as equals. In a city, parks are as essential to the physical and emotional health of a city as the water supply." He notes this is

81

not obvious from most city budgets, where parks are deemed a luxury. By contrast, "roads, the public space for cars, receive infinitely more resources and less budget cuts than parks, the public space for children. Why," he asks, "are the public spaces for cars deemed more important than the public spaces for children?"

5   Now government planners everywhere are experimenting, seeking ways to design cities for people not cars. Cars promise mobility, and they provide it in a largely rural setting. But in an urbanizing world there is an inherent conflict between the automobile and the city. After a point, as their numbers multiply, automobiles provide not mobility but immobility. Congestion also takes a direct economic toll in rising costs in time and gasoline. And urban air pollution, often from automobiles, claims millions of lives.

6   Another cost of cities that are devoted to cars is a psychological one, a deprivation of contact with the natural world—an "asphalt complex." There is a growing body of evidence that there is an innate human need for contact with nature. Both ecologists and psychologists have been aware of this for some time. Ecologists, led by Harvard University biologist E.O. Wilson, have formulated the "biophilia hypothesis," which argues that those who are deprived of contact with nature suffer psychologically and that this deprivation leads to a measurable decline in well-being.

7   Throughout the modern era, budget allocations for transportation in most countries—and in the United States, in particular—have been heavily biased toward the construction and maintenance of highways and streets. Creating more livable cities and the mobility that people desire depends on reallocating budgets to emphasize the development of rail- or bus-based public transport and bicycle support facilities.

8   The exciting news is that there are signs of change, daily indications of an interest in redesigning cities for people, not for cars. One encouraging trend comes from the United States. Public transit ridership nationwide rising by 2.1 percent a year since 1996 indicates that people are gradually abandoning their cars for buses, subways, and light rail. Rising gasoline prices are encouraging still more commuters to abandon their cars and take the bus or subway or get on a bicycle.

9   When Beijing decided to promote an automobile-centered transportation system, a group of eminent scientists in China protested. They pointed out that the country does not have enough land to accommodate the automobile and to feed its people. What is true for China is also true for India and dozens of other densely populated developing countries.

10 Some cities are far better at planning their growth than others. They plan transport systems that provide mobility, clean air, and exercise—a sharp contrast to cities that offer congestion, unhealthy air, and little opportunity for exercise. When 95 percent of a city's

workers depend on the automobile for commuting, as in Atlanta, Georgia, the city is in trouble.

11   By contrast, in Amsterdam only 40 percent of workers commute by car; 35 percent bike or walk, while 25 percent use public transit. Copenhagen's commuting patterns are almost identical to Amsterdam's. In Paris, just under half of commuters rely on cars. Even though these European cities are older, with narrow streets, they have far less congestion than Atlanta.

12   Not surprisingly, car-dependent cities have more congestion and less mobility than those that offer a wider range of commuting options. The very vehicle whose great promise was personal mobility is in fact virtually immobilizing entire urban populations, making it difficult for rich and poor alike to move about.

13   Existing long-term transportation strategies in many developing countries assume that everyone will one day be able to own a car. Unfortunately, given the constraints of land available for cars, not to mention those imposed by oil reserves, this is simply not realistic. These countries will provide more mobility if they support public transportation and the bicycle.

(Words: 1097)

Exercise I Discussion

Directions: Please discuss the following questions in pairs or groups.

1. Do you agree with the author's opinion? Why or why not?
2. Are you satisfied with the present design of transportation or other public facilities in Beijing? Which city do you think is best in its city-design in China or in other countries?
3. What should the government as well as the citizens do to make our city life better in the future?

Exercise II Writing

Directions: How do you feel about the many challenges that threaten the development of human society, such as environmental pollution, deluge of crimes, overpopulation, etc? What's your view on the future of human society, especially the future of China? Do you agree that happiness of the people rather than faster economic growth should be set as the top national goal? Write a composition on one of these questions in about 150 words.

UNIT SEVEN

HUMAN IMPACT ON NATURE

Target of the Unit

☞ To get a glimpse of how human activities, especially new technology, have impacted the world we live in
☞ To practice reading skills
☞ To enlarge your vocabulary

1) LEAD IN

Directions: In this unit, you will read 3 passages about the relationship between man and nature. They may shed some new light on your understanding of the role of man in this world. We have obviously done too much to Mother Nature, and there is still a lot more for us to do if we want to secure a brighter future for the human race. Try to relate the messages conveyed in the articles to the crises we have yet to tackle day by day.

2) DISCUSSION

Will technology change our future life for better or for worse?

Text A

After We Are Gone

By Jerry Adler

Warming-up Exercises

☞ In your imagination, what would happen when the doomsday comes?
☞ Do you believe that humans can be evacuated to outer space?

• First reading •

Directions: Now please read the following passage as fast as you can and then get the exercises done as required.

1
The Second Coming may be the most widely anticipated **apocalypse** ever, but it's far from the only version of the end times. Environmentalists have their own **eschatology**—a vision of  a world not consumed by holy fire but returned to ecological balance by the removal of the most **disruptive** species in history. That, of course, would be us, the 6 billion furiously **metabolizing** and reproducing human beings polluting its surface. There's even a group trying to bring it about, the Voluntary Human Extinction Movement, whose Web site calls on people to stop having children altogether. And now the journalist Alan Weisman has produced, if not a bible, at least a Book of **Revelation**, "The World without Us," which conjures up a future something like... well, like the area around Chernobyl, the Russian nuclear reactor that blew off a cloud of radioactive steam in 1986. In a **radius** of 30 kilometers, there are no human settlements—just forests that have begun reclaiming fields and towns, home to birds, deer, wild **boar** and **moose**.

2
Weisman's intriguing thought experiment is to ask what would happen if the rest of the Earth was similarly evacuated—not by a nuclear **holocaust** or natural disaster, but by whisking people off in spaceships, or killing them

apocalypse *n.* revelation（esp of knowledge from God）天启
eschatology *n.* branch of theology concerned with the end of the world and God's judgment of mankind after death 末世论
disruptive *adj.* interrupting usual order or progress 打乱正常秩序或进程的
metabolize *v.* to subject a substance to metabolism or produce a substance by metabolism 新陈代谢
Revelation *n.* the last book of the *New Testament*, also called *The Revelation of Saint John the Divine*《启示录》(《圣经·新约》的最后一卷)
radius *n.* （circular area measured by the）straight line from the center of a circle to any point on its circumference 半径（范围）
boar *n.* an uncastrated male pig; wild pig 公猪，野猪
moose *n.pl.* a hoofed mammal (*Alces alces*) found in forests of northern North America and in Eurasia and having a broad, pendulous muzzle and large, palmate antlers in the male 驼鹿
holocaust *n.* large-scale destruction 浩劫; the Holocaust—the genocide of European Jews and others by the Nazis during World War II; a massive slaughter 大屠杀

with a virus that spares the rest of the biosphere. In a world with no one to put out fires, repair dams or plow fields, what would become of the immense infrastructure humans have woven across the globe? In a matter of days or weeks, nuclear power plants around the world would boil off their water and melt into vast radioactive lumps. Electrical power would fail, and with it the pumps keeping New York City's subways from flooding; in a few years Lexington Avenue would collapse and eventually turn into a river. Lightning-caused fires would blow out the windows in skyscrapers, and concrete floors would freeze and buckle. A few centuries on, steel bridges would fall victim to rust and the inexorable assault of vegetation taking root in windblown clumps of soot. Masonry structures would last the longest, although the next ice age would wipe them out, at least at the latitude of New York, and bronze sculpture, Weisman estimates, would still be recognizable 10 million years into the future, probably the last recognizable artifacts of our civilization.

3   And what of the biosphere? Unless global warming has already progressed beyond the point of no return, it would eventually recover much of its diversity and richness. Contrary to widespread belief, cockroaches would not take over the world if there were no one around to step on them: tropical insects, they wouldn't survive their first winter without central heating. Rats and dogs would miss us the most, it seems—the former for our garbage and the latter our protection from bigger predators. Feral cats, on the other hand, would do quite well: there would be plenty of birds for them to eat. Elephants would once again have the run of Africa, and the oceans would be filled with fish as few alive have ever seen them. Much of the world would come to resemble... well, the Korean demilitarized zone, where no one has set foot for more than half a century, now a Mecca for Korean bird watchers.

> **biosphere** *n.* the part of the earth and its atmosphere in which living organisms exist or that is capable of supporting life 生物圈
> **buckle** *v.* to crumple or bend 弯曲，变形；垮塌
> **masonry** *n.* building that is made of stone and mortar; stonework 砖石建筑；砖石结构
> **cockroach** *n.* any of numerous oval, flat-bodied insects of the family Blattidae, including several species that are common household pests 蟑螂
> **feral** *n.* (of animals) wild or savage, esp after escaping from captivity or from life as a pet（指动物）野的，凶猛的（尤指逃脱者）
> **Mecca** *n.* spiritual center of Islam; place that very many people wish to visit（伊斯兰圣城）麦加；胜地

4   Sound appealing? Well, it did to Weisman, too, when he began work on the book four years ago. And "four out of five" of the people he's told about it, he estimates, thought the idea sounded wonderful. Since we're headed inexorably toward an environmental crash anyway, why not get it over cleanly and allow the world to heal? Over time, though, Weisman's attitude toward the rest of humanity softened, as he thought of some of the beautiful things human beings have accomplished, their architecture and poetry, and he eventually arrived at what he

views as a compromise position: a worldwide, voluntary agreement to limit each human couple to one child. This, says Weisman—who is 60, and childless after the death of his only daughter—would stabilize the human population by the end of the century at about 1.6 billion, approximately where it was in 1900. And then, perhaps, more of the world could resemble... Varosha, the beach resort in Cyprus in the no man's land between the Greek and Turkish zones, where, Weisman writes, thickets of **hibiscus**, **oleander** and passion lilac grow wild and houses disappear under **magenta** mounds of **bougainvillea**.

> **hibiscus** *n.* *Hibiscus*, or rosemallow, is a large genus of about 200-220 species of flowering plants in the family Malvaceae (the mallow family, along with members like cocoa, cotton, okra, baobab and durian) native to warm temperate, subtropical and tropical regions throughout the world. The genus includes both annual and perennial herbaceous plants, and woody shrubs and small trees. 木槿
> **oleander** *n.* a poisonous Eurasian evergreen shrub (*Nerium oleander*) having fragrant white, rose, or purple flowers, whorled leaves, and long follicles containing numerous comose seeds; also called rosebay 夹竹桃
> **magenta** *n.* bright purplish red 洋红色
> **bougainvillea** *n.* any of several South American woody shrubs or vines of the genus *Bougainvillea* having groups of three petallike, showy, variously colored bracts attached to the flowers 九重葛

5   Too bad there's no one there to see it.

(Words: 789)

· Second Reading ·

Directions: Read the text again more carefully to find enough information for Exercises I, II & III.

Exercise I True or False

Directions: Please state whether the following statements are true or not (T/F) according to the text.

1. The Second Coming may be the only version of the end times.
2. Environmentalists believed ecological balance can be only achieved by the removal of human beings.
3. Some environmental extremists called on people to stop bearing children.
4. In a radius of 30 kilometers around Chernobyl, there are neither human settlements nor forests.
5. If the rest of the Earth was similarly evacuated, steel bridges would last the longest.

6. Weisman estimates bronze sculpture would still be recognizable 10 million years into the future.

7. According to widespread belief, cockroaches would take over the world if there were no one around to step on them.

8. The Korean demilitarized zone is now a Mecca for Korean bird watchers for it is a holy place.

9. When Weisman began work on the book four years ago, "one out of five" of the people he's told about it, he estimates, didn't think the idea sounded wonderful.

10. Weisman's attitude toward the rest of humanity remained tough all the time.

Exercise II   Word Inference

Directions: Often you can guess the meaning of a word/expression by reading the words around it. Please read the given sentence to see how each word/expression in bold type is used in the text. Then choose the answer that is closest in meaning to the bold-faced word/expression.

1. …a vision of a world not **consumed** by holy fire but returned to ecological balance by the removal of the most disruptive species in history.

    A. used up   B. destroyed   C. eaten up   D. cleaned

2. And now the journalist Alan Weisman… **conjures up** a future something like… well, like the area around Chernobyl…

    A. plays magical tricks

    B. constructs

    C. causes (sth) to appear as a picture in the mind

    D. appeals solemnly to

3. …just forests that have begun **reclaiming** fields and towns, home to birds, deer, wild boar and moose.

    A. recovering possession of

    B. making (sth) suitable for cultivation

    C. reforming

    D. recycling

4. Weisman's **intriguing** thought experiment is to ask what would happen if the rest of the Earth was similarly evacuated…

    A. intricate   B. interesting   C. plotting   D. mistaken

5. ...not by a nuclear holocaust or natural disaster, but by **whisking** people **off** in spaceships, or killing them with a virus that spares the rest of the biosphere.
   A. getting rid of (sb)
   B. driving (sb) away
   C. brushing (sb) aside
   D. taking (sb) away quickly and suddenly

6. What would become of the immense **infrastructure** humans have woven across the globe?
   A. stock of fixed basic equipment (in a country)
   B. networks of communications
   C. what forms the basis of a system
   D. highway networks

7. A few centuries on, steel bridges would fall victim to rust and the inexorable assault of vegetation taking root in windblown **clumps** of soot.
   A. pieces   B. huge piles
   C. small masses   D. chunks

8. ...bronze sculpture... would still be recognizable 10 million years into the future, probably the last recognizable **artifacts** of our civilization.
   A. things made by man B. artistic works
   C. articles   D. artifice

9. Rats and dogs would miss us the most, it seems—the former for our garbage and the latter our protection from bigger **predators**.
   A. precursors   B. potential threats
   C. predecessors   D. meat-eating animals

10. Since we're headed **inexorably** toward an environmental crash anyway, why not get it over cleanly and allow the world to heal?
    A. inexcusably   B. unstoppably
    C. inexhaustibly   D. incredibly

Exercise III Discussion

Directions: Please discuss the following questions in pairs or groups.

1. Imagine what would happen if the human race were evacuated from the earth.
2. Do you think it is a way out to limit each human couple to one child?

Text B

A New Step Toward Synthetic Life

By Moises Velasquez-Manoff

Warming-up Exercises

☞ What do you know about DNA?
☞ Do you believe that scientists can design life from the ground up, and that they can choose the traits that determine what the organism eats, where it thrives, and how fast it reproduces?

First reading

Directions: Now please read the following passage as fast as you can and then get the exercises done as required.

1   Scientists have long considered DNA the instruction manual for biological life. Each species has its own unique set of instructions, or genes. And for just as long, scientists have wondered if by **swapping** these instruction manuals, they could transform one organism into another.

2   Now, in a key experiment for the **nascent** field of designing life from **scratch**, scientists at the J. Craig Venter Institute in Rockville, Md., have done just that. They have successfully transplanted the entire **genome** of one bacterium species into another, changing the recipient into an organism that looks, feels, and for all intents and purposes is, the donor.

3   "This is equivalent to changing a Macintosh computer to a PC by inserting a new piece of software," says J. Craig Venter in a **teleconference**. "Synthetic biology still remains

---

swap v. to give sth in exchange for sth else; to substitute sth for sth else 交换，替换
nascent adj. beginning to exist; not yet well developed 新生的，新兴的
scratch n. (start sth) from scratch: to begin sth without using anything that existed or was prepared before 从零开始，从头开始
genome n. the total genetic content contained in a haploid set of chromosomes in eukaryotes, in a single chromosome in bacteria, or in the DNA or RNA of viruses; an organism's genetic material [生]基因组，染色体组
teleconference n. It is the live exchange and mass articulation of information among persons and machines remote from one another but linked by a telecommunications system, usually over the phone line. It differs from videophone in intending to serve groups rather than individuals. The telecommunications system may support the teleconference by providing one or more of the following audio, video, and/or data services by one or more means, such as telephone, telegraph, teletype, radio, and television. 电话会议，视频会议

JAMES D. WATSON

to be proven, but now we are much closer to knowing it's absolutely theoretically possible."

4   The young field of synthetic biology rests on the premise that scientists can design life from the ground up, that they can choose the traits that determine what the organism eats, where it thrives, and how fast it reproduces.

5   __A__. They might be engineered to create cheap biofuels from a great variety of crops and biomass, including woody material that today is too expensive to convert profitably. They might clean up chemical spills, oil spills, and other man-made environmental disasters.

6   But the question has always lingered: Does DNA alone define an organism or do other elements factor in? The study, published Thursday in the online version of the journal Science, appears to answer that question, at least for simple bacteria known as mycoplasma.

7   "Just the chromosome itself, without any accessory proteins, is all that is necessary to boot up this cell system," says Dr. Venter. "That's a very important finding for the future of this field.... It really simplifies the task."

8   Any tinkering with nature raises ethical questions, not to mention concerns over safety. __B__. The genome already existed and the resulting organism is identical to those found in nature. What's new is the process. And as scientists take the next logical step and move toward designing organisms completely from scratch, these questions of safety and ethics will move to the fore.

> biomass *n.* It refers to living and recently dead biological material that can be used as fuel or for industrial production. Most commonly, biomass refers to plant matter grown to generate electricity or produce biofuel, but it also includes plant or animal matter used for production of fibers, chemicals or heat. Biomass may also include biodegradable wastes that can be burnt as fuel. It excludes organic material which has been transformed by geological processes into substances such as coal or petroleum. 生物质
> chromosome *n.* Chromosomes are organized structures of DNA and proteins that are found in cells. A chromosome is a singular piece of DNA, which contains many genes, regulatory elements and other nucleotide sequences. Chromosomes also contain DNA-bound proteins, which serve to package the DNA and control its functions. [生物]染色体
> denucleate *v.* to deprive of the nucleus 除去(原子、细胞等的)核

9   For decades, scientists have known that bacteria, which, unlike plants and animals, lack a defined nucleus, can freely swap genes. And Dolly, the sheep cloned in 1996, showed that a nucleus taken from one cell and implanted into another denucleated cell could grow into a viable animal. __C__.

10   "People would have predicted this would be possible based on what we know," says Philip Green, a professor of genome sciences at the University of Washington in Seattle, when informed of the project. "But you never know until you do it that it's going to work."

11 Led by microbiologist John Glass, the researchers took DNA from **mycoplasma mycoides**, a small bacterium found in goat **intestines**, and introduced it into the body of a close relative, **mycoplasma capricolum**. About one in 150,000 took. Mycoplasmas have a small number of genes—aroud 500—and no cell walls, which makes introducing DNA easier. The bacterium's simplicity also makes it a good place to begin determining the minimum instruction set, or genes, needed to create life, an important step in future attempts at designing life from the ground up.

12 While other researchers hail the technical achievement, they question the benefits of a build-from-scratch approach. When looking to design a useful organism, cost is the No.1 concern, says George Church, professor of genetics at Harvard Medical School. **D** .

13 "It's sort of like saying, 'If we could pull Manhattan to the ground and build a whole new set of skyscrapers, it would be better.' And maybe it would be. But it's expensive," he says. "I can think of lots of ways of improving Manhattan, but they don't include changing 100 percent; they include changing 1 percent."

14 When trying to create organisms that can more efficiently produce biofuels—turning woody matter into alcohol or gasoline-like compounds—nature already offers plenty of starting points, says Church—like the common **E. coli**.

15 "They need to show that this is cheaper or faster or something. And this paper doesn't do that," he says.

16 The study is an important academic achievement, but it's not critical to moving from fossil fuels to renewable biofuels, says Stephen del Cardayre, vice president of research and development at LS9 Inc., a San Carlos, Calif., company developing organisms to make biofuels. "There is much lower-hanging fruit."

17 Biofuels face several hurdles. **E**   To meet that challenge, researchers are looking at

---

mycoplasma mycoides *n.phr.* Mycoplasma is a genus of small bacteria which lack cell walls. Mycoplasma m. spp. mycoides is best known as the cause of bovine contagious pleuropneumonia (CBPP), a highly destructive disease in bovine cattle that is the only bacterial disease included in the World Organization for Animal Health's A-list of prioritised communicable animal diseases. 丝状支原体

intestine *n.* In anatomy, the intestine is the segment of the alimentary canal extending from the stomach to the anus and, in humans and other mammals, consists of two segments, the small intestine and the large intestine. In humans, the small intestine is further subdivided into the duodenum, jejunum and ileum while the large intestine is subdivided into the cecum and colo. 肠

mycoplasma capricolum *n.phr.* It belongs to the genus Mycoplasma, which is a genus of bacteria that does not have cell wall or murein. This spherical organism is distinguished from other bacteria by its small size (a characteristic of the genus Mycoplasma) and requirement of cholesterol for growth. However, its DNA structure suggests that Mycoplasma capricolum is derivative of Gram-positive bacteria. Though hard to isolate, this microorganism still can be obtained from lungs and pleural fluid of affected animals in necropsy and is readily cultured in cholesterol and serum-containing medium. 山羊支原体

E.coli *n.* Escherichia coli is one of several types of bacteria that normally inhabit the intestine of humans and animals (commensal organism). Some strains of *E.coli* are capable of causing disease under certain conditions when the immune system is compromised or disease may result from an environmental exposure. [拉]大肠（杆）菌

microorganisms that could turn biomass into fuel more efficiently than today's processes.

18   With a few modifications, existing organisms can be designed to achieve these goals, says Dr. del Cardayre, adding that LS9 is about a year away from releasing its own "renewable petroleum" from a modified organism. "I don't need a synthetic organism to do that," he says.

(Words: 898)

Second Reading

Directions: Read the text again more carefully to find enough information for Exercises I, II, III, IV & V.

Exercise I Understanding Text Organization

Directions: You may find there are a few sentences (segments) missing from the passage. Read the article through and decide where the following sentences should go.

1. But never before have scientists taken a species' naked DNA, without accessory proteins, and successfully put it into a different species, transforming it in the process.
2. The most obvious: they must be price-competitive with petroleum products.
3. But in this case scientists didn't create a truly new organism, Venter argues.
4. And starting from zero is the costliest approach.
5. Organisms engineered entirely by human hand could have wide-ranging applications.

Exercise II Multiple-Choice Questions

Directions: Please choose the best answer from the four choices given.

1. By transplanting the entire genome of one bacterium species into another, scientists have proved that _____.
   A. we can change a Macintosh computer to a PC by inserting a new piece of software
   B. synthetic biology has already been proven
   C. we can change the recipient into an organism the same as the donor
   D. synthetic organisms are easy to create
2. Which one is NOT among the wide-ranging applications of organisms engineered entirely by human hand?

A. Creating cheap biofuels.

B. Creating woody material.

C. Cleaning up chemical spills.

D. Cleaning up man-made environmental disasters.

3. "And as scientists take the next logical step and move toward designing organisms completely from scratch, these questions of safety and ethics will *move to the fore*." Which one explains the italicized expression?

   A. Become prominent.   B. Move forward.

   C. Come as an enemy.   D. Fade away.

4. What is the significance of Dolly?

   A. It is the first cloned animal.

   B. It showed that a nucleus taken from one cell and implanted into another denucleated cell, could grow into a viable animal.

   C. Dolly proved cloning is theoretically applicable.

   D. All of the above.

5. Other researchers question the benefits of the approach of this technical achievement because _____.

   A. it's too costly

   B. existing organisms can be modified to achieve the same goals

   C. both A and B

   D. they are rather jealous of those successful scientists

Exercise III   Word Matching

Directions: Please choose the supplied words to explain the original forms of the boldfaced words in the following sentences.

   A. additional   B. obstacle   C. alteration   D. hypothesis   E. acclaim

1. The young field of synthetic biology rests on the **premise** that scientists can design life from the ground up.

2. Just the chromosome itself, without any **accessory** proteins, is all that is necessary to boot up this cell system…

3. While other researchers **hail** the technical achievement…

4. Biofuels face several **hurdles**.

5. With a few **modifications**, existing organisms can be designed to achieve these goals…

Exercise IV Short-Answer Questions

Directions: Please answer the following questions briefly in your own words.

1. What might be the prospect for biofuels?
2. Why did the researchers choose mycoplasma to conduct their research?
3. Stephen del Cardayre says, "There is much lower-hanging fruit." What does he mean?

Exercise V Discussion

Directions: Please discuss the following questions in pairs or groups.

1. Discuss the pros and cons of synthetic organisms.
2. Do you want to have yourself cloned if possible? Why?/Why not?

Text C

Can We Save the World by 2015?

By Bryan Walsh

1   If international leaders were as united as the scientific community on climate change, warming might be a thing of the past. This year the UN's Nobel Prize-winning Intergovernmental Panel on Climate Change (IPCC) released a series of reports that laid to rest any doubts that global warming is real—and outlined the frightening consequences of continued inaction. At the release of the IPCC's final summary last month, UN Secretary-General Ban Ki Moon—who has made climate change a top priority of his administration—laid out the threat in stark terms. "The world's scientists have spoken clearly, and with one voice," he said. "I expect the world's policymakers to act the same."

2   Unfortunately, the global political community is a long way from speaking with one voice on anything, and climate change is no exception. We'll know for sure next week, when environment and energy ministers from around the world meet on the Indonesian island of Bali, for the UN's climate change conference. The summit has been held nearly every year since 1992, when the United Nations Framework Convention on Climate Change (UNFCC)—the document that has since guided international work on global warming—was hammered

out. It was at the 1997 conference, held in Japan, that the Kyoto Protocol was passed, but since then, there's been little progress, thanks in no small part to President George W. Bush's determined foot dragging on climate change.

3　　But with the Kyoto set to go into effect in 2008, this year's talks in Bali will be the most important international environmental negotiations in over a decade. The Kyoto Protocol—which requires developed nations who have ratified the deal to cut their greenhouse gas emissions by an average of about 5% below 1990 levels by 2012—expires in just five years. Given how long international treaties take to be developed and ratified, the world needs to begin immediately at Bali the process of preparing a successor to Kyoto to be ready by the end of 2012—otherwise, we'll be faced with a global vacuum at the very moment when greenhouse emissions must begin falling in order to avoid dangerous climate change. "It's really critical to get negotiations formally started," says David Doniger, the policy director of the Natural Resource Defense Council's climate center. "We're almost at the point of no return. If we don't turn these emission trends down soon, we're cooked."

4　　The good news is that the White House is seemingly the only place green hasn't gone mainstream. Just last week, 150 top global corporations—including General Electric, Johnson & Johnson and Shell—endorsed a petition calling for mandatory cuts in greenhouse gas emissions, a business position unthinkable just a year ago. Australia—a Kyoto holdout, like the U.S.—just elected a new Prime Minister with a strong environmental record who says he'll ratify the Protocol. States and cities in the U.S. have taken their own steps on climate change in the absence of action from the White House, and Congress is finally ready to step

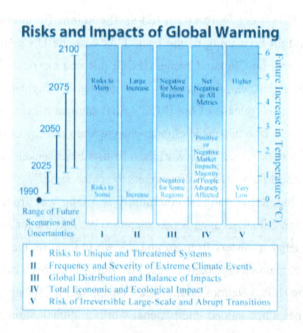

in; representatives just hammered out the details of a bill raising automobile fuel economy standards to 35 mpg. "The tenor seems to be different this time," says Jennifer Haverkamp, international counsel for Environmental Defense. "There is a building sense that enough time has been wasted and it is time to act."

5   One major dispute could trip up progress at Bali, however. Under Kyoto, only developed countries were required to make mandatory cuts in their carbon emissions; developing nations like China and India had no such demands. The U.S. has long maintained that it won't sign onto a new deal unless the developing countries are included in a more substantive way—a position unlikely to change even when the occupant of the White House does. Beijing and New Delhi both argue that the vast majority of historical carbon emissions came from the developed nations (CO_2 stays in the air for up to 200 years), so action should come from the rich first—a contention arguably supported by the UNFCCC itself, which calls for "common but differentiated responsibilities" between nations on climate change. But the reality is that the bulk of future CO_2 emissions will come from rapidly growing developing nations, and a climate deal that gave them a free pass would be useless. "We need a process that opens the door for negotiations for all economies," says Eileen Claussen, president of the Pew Center on Global Climate Change.

6   None of this will actually be decided at Bali. Despite the fact that we are rapidly running out of time to cap carbon emissions—the head of the IPCC has said the world has until 2015 at the latest—Bali is just the beginning of the beginning, not the end. As Claussen points out, a successful summit would be one that, counterintuitively, leaves much undecided—while attaching a firm deadline to the end of negotiations, with 2010 as the latest possible date. With the Bush Administration nearing lame duck status, a 2010 deadline would give a new U.S. Administration time—though not much time—to enter the process and hopefully take a leading position. That extra time might also allow China or India to soften their negotiating tactics, and perhaps accept lesser limitations, such as mandatory targets in energy efficiency or renewable power use. The best contribution President Bush can make for the Bali process is to continue doing what he has done best on climate change: nothing.

7   The whole process can seem frustratingly slow, considering how dire the threat of climate change is—as if we were convening a town hall meeting to decide to put out a fire that is already raging. "Getting 185 countries around a negotiating table is a difficult way to run the world," says Andrew Deutz, who heads the Nature Conservancy's International Institutions and Agreements team. "But the advantage of the UN process is that it's about the process. It can continue to evolve." That's already begun to happen in recent years, as consensus on global warming has grown in every corner of the world, as businesses have turned to

alternative power and governments have begun to set their own caps on carbon. But we're in a race and we're already behind. If we can't get off to a good start at Bali, we may never catch up.

(Words: 1059)

Exercise I Discussion

Directions: Please discuss the following questions in pairs or groups.

1. What do you know about global warming? Who should take more responsibility in reducing greenhouse gas emissions?
2. Do you think the quarreling countries can reach real consensus and work together to save ourselves by 2015? Why/Why not?
3. What shall we do as individuals in our own daily lives to avoid the doomsday?

Exercise II Writing

Directions: All the articles in this unit are concerned with the impact of human activities on nature, especially how technology will affect our own future. Write a composition about your personal concerns over one aspect of high-tech and its relationship with the future of humanity in about 150 words.

GLOSSARY

A

abject	*adj.*	being of the most miserable kind; wretched 绝望无助的，凄苦可怜的
accessory	*n.*	sth nonessential but desirable that contributes to an effect or result 辅助的
addiction-prone	*adj.*	addiction: compulsive physiological and psychological need for a habit-forming substance 成瘾，嗜好；prone: having a tendency or inclination, being likely 容易，易成为；合起来的意思就是 "容易上瘾"
adman	*n.*	(*infml*) a person who produces commercial advertisements 广告人
adorn	*v.*	to decorate; increase the beauty of 装饰，美化
aggravation	*n.*	annoyance; irritation 激怒，惹恼
alacrity	*n.*	speed or quickness; celerity 敏捷，轻快，迅速
alleviate	*v.*	to make (pain, for example) more bearable 减轻
allude	*v.*	to mention something or someone indirectly 影射，暗指
anonymous	*adj.*	having an unknown or unacknowledged name 无名的
apocalypse	*n.*	revelation (esp of knowledge from God) 天启
arsenic	*n.*	symbol As, a highly poisonous metallic element 符号 As, 砷：一种有剧毒的金属元素
artifacts	*n.*	something made by human beings, such as a tool or a work of art 文物
ascent	*n.*	rise 崛起
assimilation	*n.*	(process of) making sb become part of another social group or state 同化（的过程）
at large	*prep. phr.*	as a whole; in general 全体，普遍地

B

baby boomer	*n. phr.*	It is a term used to describe a person who was born during the Post-World War II baby boom between 1946 and 1964. Following World War II, several English-speaking countries—the United States, Canada, Australia, and New Zealand—experienced an unusual spike in birth rates, a phenomenon commonly referred to as the baby boom. 婴儿潮年代出生的孩子
banishment	*n.*	the action of driving sb/sth away 驱除

bar	*n.*	a standard, expectation, or degree of requirement 标准
bemoan	*v.*	to express grief over 表示悲哀; to express disapproval of or regret for 表示不同意
bestride	*v.*	(fml) to sit or stand with one leg on each side of (sth) 两腿分开跨坐/站在(某物)上
biomass	*n.*	It refers to living and recently dead biological material that can be used as fuel or for industrial production. Most commonly, biomass refers to plant matter grown to generate electricity or produce biofuel, but it also includes plant or animal matter used for production of fibers, chemicals or heat. Biomass may also include biodegradable wastes that can be burnt as fuel. It excludes organic material which has been transformed by geological processes into substances such as coal or petroleum. 生物质
biosphere	*n.*	the part of the earth and its atmosphere in which living organisms exist or that is capable of supporting life 生物圈
BlackBerry	*n.*	The BlackBerry solution consists of smartphones integrated with software that enables access to email and other communication services. 黑莓手机
blatant	*adj.*	very obvious; unashamed 明目张胆的
blender	*n.*	liquidizer 榨汁机
bloat	*v.*	to become swollen or inflated 使肿胀，变肿或膨胀
boar	*n.*	an uncastrated male pig; wild pig 公猪，野猪
bookie	*n.*	someone whose job is to collect money that people want to risk on the result of a race, competition etc, and who pays them if they guess correctly 赌注登记经纪人
bottom line	*n. phr.*	(infml) deciding or crucial factor 决定性因素; essential point (in an argument, etc) (论辩等的)基本论点，根本问题
bougainvillea	*n.*	any of several South American woody shrubs or vines of the genus *Bougainvillea* having groups of three petallike, showy, variously colored bracts attached to the flowers 九重葛
bravado	*n.*	(usu unnecessary or false) display of boldness 逞能；虚张声势
buckle	*v.*	to crumple or bend 弯曲，变形；垮塌
bump into	*v. phr.*	to meet by chance 偶遇
buzz	*n.*	rumor; gossip 流言

C

capsize	*v.*	to overturn or cause to overturn 倾覆或引起倾覆
cargo	*n.*	(load of) goods carried in a ship or aircraft (船/飞机运载的)货物(量)
catchy	*adj.*	easily remembered 好记的
chalk sth up	*v. phr.*	to record what one has done; to write sth down (usu with chalk) 记录下来，记上一笔
chromosome	*n.*	Chromosomes are organized structures of DNA and proteins that are found

in cells. A chromosome is a singular piece of DNA, which contains many genes, regulatory elements and other nucleotide sequences. Chromosomes also contain DNA-bound proteins, which serve to package the DNA and control its functions. [生物]染色体

churn	v.	to move about vigorously or violently 剧烈翻腾
clump	n.	a clustered mass; a lump 块
cockroach	n.	any of numerous oval, flat-bodied insects of the family Blattidae, including several species that are common household pests 蟑螂
coddle	v.	to treat indulgently 溺爱
concede	v.	to acknowledge, often reluctantly, as being true, just, or proper; admit (勉强)承认
conceited	adj.	self-important, proud 自傲，骄傲
conjure up	v. phr.	to call or bring to mind; evoke (引起)想象
creationism	n.	the position that the account of the creation of the universe given at the beginning of the Bible is literally true 特创论：认为《圣经》篇首给出的创造宇宙的叙述是真实无误的学说
curb	v.	to check, restrain, or control as if with a curb; rein in 遏制，阻止
curriculum	n.	all the courses of study offered by an educational institution 全部课程
cushion	n.	something that mitigates or relieves an adverse effect 缓解，缓冲
cutting edge	n.	the newest and most exciting stage in the development of something 前沿
Cyclops	n.	any of the three one-eyed Titans who forged thunderbolts for Zeus 泰坦神(为宙斯制造雷电的三个独眼泰坦神之一)

D

dash	n.	small amount of sth added or mixed 少量掺合物或混合物
daunting	adj.	intimidating 使畏惧的
decadent	adj.	corrupt, depraved, debauched 腐败的，腐朽的
demographic	n.	of a part of the population that is considered as a group, especially by advertisers who want to sell things to that group 特定人群
denucleate	v.	to deprive of the nucleus 除去(原子、细胞等的)核
differentiator	n.	sth that distinguishes one thing/person from the other 区分者，差别指数
discernible	adj.	perceptible, as by the faculty of vision or the intellect 看得清,辨别得出的
disruptive	adj.	interrupting usual order or progress 打乱正常秩序或进程的
disseminate	v.	to spread abroad; promulgate 传播
dogma	n.	a doctrine or system of doctrines proclaimed by authority as true 教条
dumb down	v.phr.	(used to show disapproval) to present news or information in a simple and attractive way without many details so that everyone can understand it 为求通俗易懂而将内容简单化(用于表示不赞同)

E

E. coli	*n.*	Escherichia coli is one of several types of bacteria that normally inhabit the intestine of humans and animals (commensal organism). Some strains of *E. coli* are capable of causing disease under certain conditions when the immune system is compromised or disease may result from an environmental exposure. [拉]大肠(杆)菌
embargo	*n.*	official order that forbids sth, esp trade, the movement of ships, etc 禁运
emeritus	*adj.*	retired but retaining an honorary title corresponding to that held immediately before retirement 荣誉退休的, 退休但仍荣誉保持退休前所拥有的职位
empathetic	*adj.*	showing empathy or ready comprehension of others' states 同情的
encompass	*v.*	to constitute or include 包含
encore	*n.*	an additional performance in response to the demand of an audience 再来一次
endemic	*adj.*	an endemic disease or problem is always present in a particular place, or among a particular group of people 地方性的, 某一人群所特有的
engrossed	*adj.*	giving or marked by complete attention to 全神贯注的, 精神集中的
entry-level job	*n. phr.*	a job appropriate for or accessible to one who is inexperienced in a field or new to a market 入门水平工作, 低级别工作
eschatology	*n.*	branch of theology concerned with the end of the world and God's judgment of mankind after death 末世论
exacerbate	*v.*	to make a bad situation worse 加剧, 恶化
exhilarating	*adj.*	exciting, thrilling 令人激动的

F

feral	*n.*	(of animals) wild or savage, esp after escaping from captivity or from life as a pet (指动物)野的, 凶猛的(尤指逃脱者)
ferocious	*adj.*	fierce, violent or savage 残忍的, 凶猛的, 野蛮的
filet mignon	*n.*	(US) small tender piece of beef without bones, cut from a sirloin (牛的)里脊
filter	*n.*	a device containing porous materials, especially one used to extract impurities from air or water 过滤装置
fizzle	*v.*	(infml) to fail or end weakly, especially after a hopeful beginning 失败, 夭折, 尤指开始时很有希望但最终失败或结局不好
flask	*n.*	a small container, such as a bottle, having a narrow neck and usually a cap 水瓶
flip-flops	*n.*	In footwear and fashion, flip-flops (also known as thongs, jandals, slippers, or pluggers) are a flat, backless, usually rubber sandal consisting of a flat sole held loosely on the foot by a Y-shaped strap, like a thin thong, that passes between the first (big) and second toes and around either side of

the foot. They appear to have been developed based on traditional Japanese woven or wooden soled sandals. 夹趾拖鞋

flourish	v.	to do or fare well; prosper 繁荣，进行得好
frothing	adj.	producing froth; (infml) extremely angry 口吐白沫的，极其愤怒的

G

gall	n.	outrageous insolence; effrontery 厚脸皮
gauge	v.	to measure precisely 精确地测量
gazillion(s)	n.	(infml) an indefinitely large number 极大数目
generic	adj.	relating to or descriptive of an entire group or class 类的；通用的，普遍的
genome	n.	the total genetic content contained in a haploid set of chromosomes in eukaryotes, in a single chromosome in bacteria, or in the DNA or RNA of viruses; an organism's genetic material [生]基因组，染色体组
glamorization	n.	the act of glamorizing; making sth or someone more beautiful (often in a superficial way) 美化
goombah	n.	a companion or an associate, especially an older friend who acts as a patron, a protector, or an adviser 同伴或同事，特指以赞助人、保护人或顾问身份出现的年长的朋友
gratuitous	adj.	given or received without cost or obligation; free 无偿的，免费或无需承担义务和费用地得到或接受的
grime	n.	black dirt or soot, especially such dirt clinging to or ingrained in a surface 沉积在表面的灰尘或烟黑

H

hail	v.	to praise, acclaim, or acknowledge 欢呼
harangues	n.	a long pompous speech, especially one delivered before a gathering 慷慨激昂的长篇大论
harass	v.	to irritate or torment persistently 不断地激怒或骚扰
harmonics	n.	the theory or study of the physical properties and characteristics of musical sound 和声
hassle	v.	to argue or fight 争执
heap	v.	to bestow in abundance or lavishly 将大量的(表扬或批评)加之于……
hibiscus	n.	*Hibiscus*, or rosemallow, is a large genus of about 200–220 species of flowering plants in the family Malvaceae (the mallow family, along with members like cocoa, cotton, okra, baobab and durian) native to warm temperate, subtropical and tropical regions throughout the world. The genus includes both annual and perennial herbaceous plants, and woody shrubs and small trees. 木槿

holocaust	n.	large-scale destruction 浩劫；the Holocaust—the genocide of European Jews and others by the Nazis during World War II; a massive slaughter 大屠杀
hurdle	n.	an obstacle or difficulty to be overcome 障碍
hype	n.	misleading and exaggerated publicity 言过其实的宣传报道
hyper-anxiety	n.	the state of being over-anxious 高度紧张
hypothetically	adv.	of, relating to, or based on a hypothesis 猜想地

I

illderly	n.	those for whom health is the main focus of their lives 终生疾病缠身者
implicate	v.	to show or seem to show that sth is the cause of sth bad or harmful（仿佛）表明（某物）导致（不好或有害之事）
impropriety	n.	the quality or condition of being improper.
incubator	n.	a place or situation that permits or encourages the formation and development, as of new ideas 允许或鼓励新的想法产生并发展的地方或形式；孵化器
inexorably	adv.	not capable of being persuaded by entreaty; relentless 冷酷无情地
ingest	v.	to take into the body by the mouth for digestion or absorption 咽下
ingredient	n.	an element in a mixture or compound; a constituent 成份
inscribe	v.	to write, print, carve, or engrave (words or letters) on or in a surface. 刻,写,雕
inscrutable	adj.	difficult to fathom or understand; impenetrable 不可思议的
insinuate	v.	~oneself into sth, to place oneself smoothly and stealthily into sth 使自己悄然潜入某事物中
insouciance	n.	blithe lack of concern; nonchalance 漫不经心，漠不关心
intestine	n.	In anatomy, the intestine is the segment of the alimentary canal extending from the stomach to the anus and, in humans and other mammals, consists of two segments, the small intestine and the large intestine. In humans, the small intestine is further subdivided into the duodenum, jejunum and ileum while the large intestine is subdivided into the cecum and colo. 肠
inventory	n.	detailed list, eg of goods, furniture, jobs to be done 清单

J

jettison	v.	to cast overboard or off 抛弃或丢弃
juggle	v.	to keep (more than two activities, for example) in motion or progress at one time 兼顾几件事情，两头忙活
jump-start	v.	to help a process or activity to start or become more successful 助推，发起

K

knead	v.	to mix and work into a uniform mass, as by folding, pressing, and stretching with the hands 揉成，捏制

L

laden	adj.	loaded, weighed down （为名等）所累
laissez-faire	n.	policy of freedom from government control 自由放任政策
laughingstock	n.	an object of jokes or ridicule; a butt 玩笑或嘲弄的对象，抨击的对象，笑柄
lumber	v.	to move in a heavy clumsy way 笨重地移动

M

magenta	n.	bright purplish red 洋红色
manicure	v.	to clip or trim evenly and closely 修剪
maraud	v.	to rove and raid in search of booty 劫掠，四处流窜抢劫
margin	n.	difference between cost price and selling price 差价，利润
masonry	n.	building that is made of stone and mortar; stonework 砖石建筑；砖石结构
matriarch	n.	a woman who rules a family, clan, or tribe 女族长，女家长
Mecca	n.	spiritual center of Islam; place that very many people wish to visit (伊斯兰圣城)麦加；胜地
meerkat	n.	a small southern African mongoose, especially the suricate (南非) 海岛猫鼬
metabolize	v.	to subject a substance to metabolism or produce a substance by metabolism 新陈代谢
mire	v.	to hinder, entrap, or entangle as if in mire 使受困扰，使阻碍、牵绊或纠缠 （如陷入泥沼一般）
modification	n.	any of the changes in an organism caused by environment or activity and not genetically transmissable to offspring 改变
moose	n. pl.	a hoofed mammal (*Alces alces*) found in forests of northern North America and in Eurasia and having a broad, pendulous muzzle and large, palmate antlers in the male 驼鹿
motivator	n.	a positive motivational influence; incentive 积极推动的影响力;吸引,动因
mycoplasma capricolum	n.phr.	It belongs to the genus Mycoplasma, which is a genus of bacteria that does not have cell wall or murein. This spherical organism is distinguished from other bacteria by its small size (a characteristic of the genus Mycoplasma) and requirement of cholesterol for growth. However, its DNA structure suggests that Mycoplasma capricolum is derivative of Gram-positive bacteria. Though hard to isolate, this microorganism still can be obtained from lungs and pleural fluid of affected animals in necropsy and is

mycoplasma mycoides	n.phr.	readily cultured in cholesterol and serum-containing medium. 山羊支原体 Mycoplasma is a genus of small bacteria which lack cell walls. Mycoplasma m. spp. mycoides is best known as the cause of bovine contagious pleuropneumonia (CBPP), a highly destructive disease in bovine cattle that is the only bacterial disease included in the World Organization for Animal Health's A-list of prioritised communicable animal diseases. 丝状支原体

N

nascent	adj.	beginning to exist; not yet well developed 新生的，新兴的
neuroscience	n.	the study of the brain and nervous system, including molecular neuroscience, cellular neuroscience, cognitive neuroscience, psychophysics, computational modeling and diseases of the nervous system 神经学
newfangled	adj.	recently designed or produced 新设计的；新创的(只作定语，多表示不赞同或不信任)
nomenclature	n.	a set or system of names or terms used by an individual or community, especially those used in a particular science (scientific nomenclature) or art; naming 命名

O

oblivious	adj.	lacking conscious awareness; unmindful 不知不觉的，不自觉的
oleander	n.	a poisonous Eurasian evergreen shrub (*Nerium oleander*) having fragrant white, rose, or purple flowers, whorled leaves, and long follicles containing numerous comose seeds; also called rosebay 夹竹桃
ooze	v.	(of thick liquids) come or flow out slowly (指浓稠液体)慢慢流出
opine	v.	to hold or state as an opinion 持有意见或发表意见
oxymoronic	adj.	contradictory 自相矛盾的

P

paean	n.	a fervent expression of joy or praise 赞歌，欢乐歌
particulates	n. pl.	a minute separate particle, as of a granular substance or powder 微粒
patrol	n.	the act of moving about an area especially by an authorized and trained person or group, for purposes of observation, inspection, or security 巡逻
pedagogical	adj.	of, relating to, or characteristic of pedagogy, educational 教育学的,教学法的
perdition	n.	loss of the soul; eternal damnation 毁灭，灵魂的失落，永久的罚入地狱
perpetuate	v.	to cause sth to continue 使(某事物)永久、永存或持续
pinprick	n.	sth that slightly annoys sb 小烦恼
plausible	adj.	reasonable, believable 可信的

plethora	n.	quantity greater than what is needed; over-abundance 过量，过剩
plucky	adj.	having or showing courage and spirit in trying circumstances 有勇气的,有胆量的
powerhouse	n.	(fig) very powerful group, organization, etc（比喻）强大的组织、团体等; a highly energetic and indefatigable person 干将
predator	n.	an organism that lives by preying on other organisms 掠食动物; one that victimizes, plunders, or destroys, especially for one's own gain 劫掠他人者
premise	n.	a proposition upon which an argument is based or from which a conclusion is drawn 前提
pristine	adj.	remaining free from dirt or decay; clean 新鲜的或清洁的，干净的
proliferation	n.	rapid increase in the number or amount of sth 迅速的增长；扩散
purport	v.	to have the intention of doing 有意

Q

quagmire	n.	an area of soft wet muddy ground; a difficult or complicated situation 泥沼；困境
quarter	v.	to dismember (a human body) into four parts 将(人体)肢解成四分

R

rabbi	n.	(abbr.) a person trained in Jewish law, ritual, and tradition and ordained for leadership of a Jewish congregation, especially one serving as chief religious official of a synagogue 拉比；a scholar qualified to interpret Jewish law 犹太学者
radius	n.	(circular area measured by the) straight line from the center of a circle to any point on its circumference 半径(范围)
ranger	n.	(esp US) guard who patrols and protects a forest, etc 护林员
ratchet	v.	to increase or decrease by increments 渐进，通常与up, upward, down 或 downward 一起使用
reclaim	v.	to recover possession of sth 恢复或收回某事物；to bring into or return to a suitable condition for use, as cultivation or habitation 开垦，开荒
reinforce	v.	to give more force or effectiveness to; strengthen 加强，强化
reinvigorate	v.	to give a boost, revive 振兴，使重新获得活力
restless	adj.	not able to rest, relax, or be still 坐卧不安，呆不住
retain	v.	to keep, preserve 留住
red flag	n. .	(Am.) something that shows or warms you that something might be wrong,illegal etc. 警示信号，危险信号
Revelation	n.	the last book of the *New Testament*, also called *The Revelation of Saint John the Divine* 《启示录》(《圣经·新约》的最后一卷)

rung	*n.*	cross-piece forming a step in a ladder; level or rank in society, one's career, an organization, etc 梯级，等级
rut	*n.*	deep track made by a wheel or wheels in soft ground; furrow 车辙

S

sacrilege	*n.*	(act of) treating a sacred thing or place with disrespect 亵渎圣物或圣地的行为
Scandinavian	*adj.*	of or relating to Scandinavia or to its peoples, languages, or cultures 斯堪的纳维亚的，其民族、语言和文化的或与之有关的
scoff	*v.*	to speak contemptuously (about or to sb/sth); jeer or mock 嘲弄，嘲笑
scratch	*n.*	(start sth) **from scratch**: to begin sth without using anything that existed or was prepared before 从零开始，从头开始
seamy	*adj.*	sordid; base 丑恶的，肮脏的，卑鄙的
shell out	*v. phr.*	to hand over; pay 支付
shuttlecock	*n.*	a small rounded piece of cork or rubber with a conical crown of feathers or plastic, used in badminton, also called bird, birdie 羽毛球
smoothie	*n.*	a thick drink made of fruit and fruit juices mixed together, sometimes with ice, milk and yoghurt 以水果、果汁及牛奶或酸奶混合而成的浓稠饮品
snobbish	*adj.*	of, befitting, or resembling a snob; pretentious 势利眼的
sod	*n.*	a fellow; a guy 家伙
soothe	*v.*	to make (a worried or angry person) calm and relaxed 安慰，安抚
splay	*v.*	to spread apart widely, or to make things, esp parts of the body, do this (尤指四肢)伸展开
sputter	*v.*	to make short soft uneven noises like very small explosions 发出噼噼啪啪声
squealer	*n.*	animal that squeals 尖声嚎叫的动物
stark	*adj.*	complete or utter; extreme 完全的；极端的
staunch	*adj.*	firm and steadfast 坚定的
swap	*v.*	to give sth in exchange for sth else; to substitute sth for sth else 交换,替换
symphony	*n.*	a consonance or harmony of sounds, agreeable to the ear, whether the sounds are vocal or instrumental, or both 交响（乐）

T

teleconference	*n.*	It is the live exchange and mass articulation of information among persons and machines remote from one another but linked by a telecommunications system, usually over the phone line. It differs from videophone in intending to serve groups rather than individuals. The telecommunications system may support the teleconference by providing one or more of the following audio, video, and/or data services by one or more means, such as telephone, telegraph, teletype, radio, and television. 电话会议，视频会议

telephonically	adv.	by telephonic means or processes; by the use of the telephone 通过使用电话
telltale	n.	sth that indicates or reveals information; a sign 流露的迹象
therapy	n.	treatment of illness or disability 治疗
throb	v.	to beat rapidly or violently, as the heart; pound 悸动，砰砰跳
tinker	v.	to work in a casual or inexpert way, esp trying to repair or improve sth 胡乱修理，乱改动，瞎鼓捣
tote	v.	(infml) to carry sth, esp regularly 携带，装备于某人身上
turf	n.	territory 地盘；lawn 草坪
turnover	n.	rate at which workers leave a factory, company, etc and replaced 人事变动率

U

unblemished	adj.	not marred or impaired by any flaw 没有瑕疵的，未被破坏的
understatement	n.	a statement that is restrained in ironic contrast to what might have been said 含蓄的表达
unencumbered	adj.	not burdened with cares or responsibilities 没有累赘的
unfettered	adj.	not limited or controlled 不受约束羁绊的
unplugged (company town)	adj.	A lot of small towns, especially in the more rural parts of the country, have only one major factory/company located nearby. These towns become very dependent on said companies, and when they move out overseas, it can be devastating for the town and surrounding areas. So, it just basically means a town that had "the" factory ripped/jerked/unplugged from the community, and has suffered a great deal.（支柱企业）彻底搬迁走的（城镇）

V

vaunt	v.	to boast about 吹嘘，夸耀
veneer	n.	superficial appearance covering/disguising the true nature of sb/sth 虚假的表象
viable	adj.	feasible, practicable 可行的
vogue	n.	fashion 潮流
volatile	adj.	tending to violence; explosive 易爆发的，爆炸性的

W

waft	n.	sth, such as an odor, that is carried through the air （气味、风等的）一股
walkie-talkie	n.	(pl) walkie-talkies; a battery-powered portable sending and receiving radio set 步话机
warts and all	n. phr.	all defects and imperfections notwithstanding 尽管有各种缺点与瑕疵

wellderly	n.	America's healthy elderly people are known as the *wellderly*—those 80 years and older with no history of chronic disease 健康老人
widget	n.	an imaginary product that a company might produce 设想中的新装置/产品
wilt	v.	(infml) to feel weak or tired, esp because one is too hot (因天热而)发蔫, 感觉疲惫
wisecracking	v. p.p.	making smart or clever remarks (often unkind) 说俏皮话, 说风凉话
wreckage	n.	remains of sth that has been wrecked or ruined (被毁坏之物的)残骸

X

xenophobia	n.	a person unduly fearful or contemptuous of that which is foreign, especially of strangers or foreign peoples 恐外症, 排外情绪

Y

yawning	adj.	gaping open 咧开大口

Z

zillion(s)	n.	very large indeterminate number 极大数目